When I was a child
 I loved to sing a song, like so:
  "This little light of mine,
 I am going to let it shine."
  As I began to grow into adulthood, with time,
 My light began to grow dimmer and dimmer,
  Until there was a little shimmer.
With a force of a strong might,
  The darkness fell on my childhood light.
There came one quiet night,
  In my bedroom, with windows tight,
A great white light.
  The light took away the darkness that night,
And led me back with delight.
  I stay close to the great white light.
Today I sing my childhood song, with all my might:
  "This little light of mine,
I am going to let it shine."
God, thank you for bringing me
  Back to the child of light.

—Sharon Cook

Return to the Child of Light

*One woman's courageous journey
out of darkness and back into light.*

by
Sharon L. Cook

with
Graciela B. Sholander

illustrated by
Carol A. Claypool

cover by
Kevin A. Sholander

Triangle Publishing House
Fort Collins, Colorado

DEDICATION

This book is to honor and thank the Christ Light for the love
that has been shown to me,
    to honor Mother for teaching me to search,
        my brother, John, for searching for his path,
        my friends and family, who have been my
        teachers in life,
        Judy for her love and support throughout these years,
        Graciela for her openness, curiosity, and belief
        in my story,
        and Kevin for his support and help with her writing,
        Carol and Michael for their encouragement,
        Larry for his love and for cheering me on,
and to honor my sons, David and Robert, who have the
courage to leave the path of darkness and take steps toward
returning to the Child of Light.
        Thank you all from my heart.

                              Love,
                              Sharon

TABLE OF CONTENTS

Acknowledgments

I want to thank the following who helped this book become a reality:

Eileen, Claudia, Cynthia, Imeldia, Graciela and Kevin, Charlton, Carol and Michael, Sherrie, Judy, Fran, Gae, Greta, Toni, Anna Raye, Marijane, Jean, Larry, my sons, my mother, and an anonymous friend—she stood beside me in my darkest hours.

Thank you all for your belief in me and for your support.

Foreword

In over thirty-five years of practice as a child counselor, educational psychologist, and college professor, I have seen a number of books documenting the lives and recovery of individuals from a variety of problems. Ms. Cook describes her own fall and restoration in vivid terms and with sensitiv ity. She weaves in personal determination, love from others, service to others, spiritual awakening, and gentleness into a fabric of triumph to tell us *we can all do this*, too.

Many of us suffer individually or collectively from the idea that we are prisoners to and of our past. We perceive our suffering and lack of ability to recover as originating at the hands of others because of their malevolence towards us, or because others have an unfair advantage, or because we belong to a particular racial or religious group, or because we have been burdened by our past wrongs and are locked in by them. Yet we readily see both in religious teachings and in the findings of modern psychology that our recovery will never occur unless we look to the present and forgive and move on with the blessings God has given us for today.

Sharon has documented this process and in so doing, has provided hope for all of us who read her story. Her account points out our need to acknowledge our personal responsibility to ourselves, to others, and to God and to recognize that there are "few victims but mostly volunteers." This recognition is not a self-condemning task but a release given to us. It is a deliverance from fear, sadness, anger, and resentment and to a self-confidence and a positive perception of our ultimate unity with creation. Sharon's story gives us a sense of comfort and knowledge that our past does not have to compel us, but it can impel us if we let go and push against it to the future! Enjoy your journey with Sharon and begin your own now, today.

—Dr. Charlton Lee, M.A.

Chapter 1
Born Of Light

Full of the light of life, I was ready to explore and learn.

When I was a baby born
     I felt I was free to explore.
I found my toes and hands,
     How nice it was to expand!
My mother and father nurtured and fed.
     I lifted my tiny head,
And later began to crawl.
     Look how many things I felt and saw!
Walking came early for me,
     I needed to explore the trees.
I had no shame. I was, naturally.
     I was important to me.
The growing process started in 1940,
     What an adventure life would be!
My mother and father had no idea,
     They thought having a child was a breeze.
They were young and so naive!
                    —Sharon Cook

I entered the world as a breech baby one foggy Southern California day in September, 1940. What a frightening world it was. Americans hadn't yet recovered from the Great Depression when they found themselves grappling with the prospect of fighting in a raging war that escalated overseas.

No wonder my parents, at the tender age of twenty-one, were being torn apart. The pain and insecurities which they brought with them from their native Arkansas to a new life in California multiplied in this climate of fear. My mother's father had passed away suddenly from pneumonia three months before her wedding. A year earlier, my father's brother was killed in a head-on car collision. These losses weighed down my parents heavily.

My arrival brought them joy. On my fifty-fourth birthday, Mother wrote to me, "You were the dearest little baby girl, so much a personality of your very own that I don't think I could ever conceive the mystery you so definitely and continuously conveyed ... the most vivid memory was the beautiful little face with a mouth like a perfect rose." My father had wanted a baby girl during the entire pregnancy and was elated when I was born. Mother says he was so proud, and she remembers him playing with me as if I was a little doll.

Eager to venture forth on my own, I took my first steps at ten months. I was a very enthusiastic and trusting youngster, curious about everything. I laughed with ease and stretched my arms out to anybody who walked by.

Mother and I were close from the beginning. She was a wonderful nurturer. I was with her everywhere she went, except for her job at a packing house which she took when I was seven months old. She bought me pretty dresses and gave me material things whenever she could afford them— not an easy thing to do in the post-depression era. Most importantly, she gave me love and companionship.

Very early on, the world was a fascinating place for me. Full of the light of life, I was ready to explore and learn. Little did I know then how darkness would begin to creep insidiously into my young life.

Chapter 2

Seeds Of Anger And Fear

My world started to fall apart like the world of 1943.

When I was a child of three
I became a sickly little girl.
My world started to fall apart
Like the world of 1943.
My mother and father lived apart,
And I lost my security.
The spontaneous little girl became
Frightened and lonely.
My mother went to work in a factory.
My father went to the service
so we would be free.
My father drank and frightened me.
　　　　　　　　　　—Sharon Cook

I know that my father loved me. But all my childhood memories of him are tinged with fear.

He was a handsome man, tall, blonde, with mischievous blue eyes and a broad smile. Mother says his personality could charm birds right out of trees. They met at a pie supper when both were seventeen, became sweethearts, and were wed at twenty. Young and in love, neither one was financially or emotionally prepared for married life far from family and long-time friends.

Father couldn't seem to settle down, nor could he keep a job for very long. He went out drinking and womanizing while mother stayed home to care for me. When she was at work, she left me with our neighbors whom I adored. In the evenings she watched over me, cooked, cleaned, shopped for groceries, and washed our clothes, with little support from my father.

Mother was busy around the clock and slept little, sleeping even less after I became a sick child plagued first by whooping cough and later by a chronic cough that lasted for years. When I was three, my tonsils were removed. At four, I caught pneumonia and the measles. Mother wasn't sure I'd survive. With help from her sisters, she took the best care of me she possibly could. Somehow I made it through all of my early childhood maladies.

While Mother was my caretaker and protector, Father was practically a stranger. After being drafted into the army, he was gone from home several months for basic training. One evening, the black-out siren had just begun to wail its lonely, mournful cry and the lights were off inside the house when my father walked through the front door.

His uniform made him seem formidable, even intimidating, to me. The pungent smell of alcohol was strong on his breath. Eager to see his child after such a long absence, my father rushed over to pick me up and then playfully threw me into the air. But I hit the wall hard and landed on a blue blanket on the bed. I screamed and shook violently, frightened nearly to death. Mother ran quickly to drape her arms around me while I continued to shiver and whimper.

When the all-clear signal sounded about an hour later and the lights came back on, I calmed down. But the episode left its imprint on most of my life. Until I was forty-five, I shook fiercely whenever I was afraid.

I was a very sensitive child. Movie scenes with Frankenstein and other monsters scared me, giving me terrible nightmares. I also absorbed my parents' insecurities. The war frightened them, and my father's alcoholism and involvement with other women generated tremendous tension in our household.

When I was three, Father left us and returned to Arkansas. He mailed divorce papers to Mother, which she signed, notarized, and sent back. That was it. Later, he showed up at our house begging Mother to remarry him. She refused. She had had enough.

So Mother and I were left to take care of each other and brave the world together. I felt her loneliness and wanted to protect her, to make her happy. I took on more and more responsibilities, like holding on to tickets for her each time we rode the bus.

And were we on the bus a lot! Those were some of the best times we shared together, riding the bus to visit my aunts on Sunday afternoons. I also lovingly recall accompanying Mother to beauty school, enjoying the cream puff she treated me to as I snuggled close to her on the bus seat.

I could talk with Mother about practically anything. Very early, she taught me about God through word and through example. She and other women in my young life were caring and nurturing. But where were the men? My father had abandoned us. Positive male role models were nowhere to be found.

A distant male cousin thought he was funny when he faked raging fits in front of me and other children. We missed the humor. He merely succeeded in scaring us out of our wits. My fear of men grew and grew. There was no man around to love me and protect me.

Then a terrible thing happened which triggered intense anger to burn in my young heart. Mother had found an older couple to take care of me while she worked as a beautician. They seemed like nice people, but the husband began to fondle me. I was five years old. His actions frightened me and made me feel guilty. I knew that what he was doing to me couldn't be normal.

The abuse went on once a week for several months until I had the courage to tell my mother. I pleaded with her to stop taking me to their house, then told her what had happened. Thankfully she believed me. She was furious at the molester, but we never saw the couple again and charges were not pressed. In those days, children's accusations weren't taken very seriously by society.

With all that was happening in my early years, church became one of my strongholds. I loved being in the sanctuary—the organ, the music, and the people captivated me. I learned to sing, "Jesus loves me, this I know, for the Bible tells me so." In times of distress, I clung to this song for comfort.

School provided another refuge. I was older than most of the other children and took care of them, helping to tie their shoes and button their coats. I had many friends, and both my kindergarten and first grade teachers made me feel important by allowing me to help correct papers.

When I was six years old, my mother remarried. She was twenty-seven, he was forty-six. Suddenly, I had a stepfather, step-grandparents, and a seventeen-year-old stepbrother. I was elated to have a new family, especially a father to love me at last. I quickly became the apple of his eye. He loved me and tried to take good care of me. But he, too, drank and scared me.

I was proud of my stepbrother, who was a handsome, popular high school football star. When I was seven, I joined the pep rally team where I cheered for him loudly. But at home he hardly spoke to me. When he did say something, I held on to his words as though they were rare gems. I couldn't figure out why he was ignoring me, and it made me feel unworthy.

Later in life, I learned that he was jealous of the attention his father was giving me. He had lost all contact with his mother. As a young teenager, he had been molested at a military school for boys. With nobody to genuinely confide in, he must have felt utterly isolated. Although he was popular in high school and enjoyed success on a semi-professional football team in his thirties, he still died at forty-one from a combination of lung cancer and the effects of alcoholism. Mother believes that sorrow was what really killed him, since he had never truly learned how to accept love.

My stepfather regarded me highly, but he was strict and demanding. Both he and my step-grandparents were very much from the old school of thought when it came to discipline. I underwent tremendous stress when my step-grandparents became my babysitters, especially with my step-grandfather dying of cancer. I was petrified each time I had to help change his blood-soaked sheets.

Whenever I said something wrong, my step-grandmother washed my mouth out with soap. Each time I misbehaved, she locked me in a dark closet. She reported my misdeeds to my stepfather, who would then beat me with a coat hanger. If he was drunk, the beatings were especially severe. I learned to pad my jeans with extra clothing so that the physical pain would be tolerable, but I couldn't shield myself from emotional suffering which accompanied the abuse.

Looking for an escape, I started to withdraw from the world in fantasy. I created loving brothers and sisters to be my imaginary playmates. In my mind, I made people kind, gentle, and caring, the way I had been taught in church that we all should be.

Sometimes I played with sow bugs and kittens, pretending I was their animal trainer. Other times I was a nurse, a dancer, or a teacher. I often imagined I was a shining star flying with all the heavenly bodies across the skies. I also imagined that God rode the clouds down to pick me up and take me with Him to beautiful, faraway meadows.

There was so much criticism in the household that I began to feel I couldn't do anything right. I had to build myself up somehow, so I pretended I was the best pie baker in town. I made pies out of mud and dandelions, selling them to invisible customers who lavished me with praise over my unsurpassed baking skills.

School and church were havens where it was safe to be my naturally outgoing self. How peaceful these places were in contrast to the turbulent home environment! I often wished I could spend all day in school.

At home I clung to my favorite doll, Joanne, and to a little bear named Teddy. I sang "Away In A Manger" to them, pretending Teddy was Baby Jesus. Joanne and Teddy were my sleeping companions because they made me feel secure, but I also acted out my hurt and anger with them. I was expressing what was being done to me, first spanking and beating them harshly, then cuddling them with remorse.

Even in the innocent world of play, my growing mistrust of people was starting to extinguish the light within me.

Chapter 3
Desperately Seeking Love

On the outside, I seemed confident and carefree, but a big part within was still the frightened, insecure little girl of three.

"Sharon and I go way back. Our first contact was when we went to kindergarten together. We again met in junior high, and became good friends in high school. We are still extremely good friends to this day, even though our lives have taken very different turns. While mine has remained stable, Sharon's life has been tumultuous. The biggest surprise I received from Sharon was when I hadn't heard from her for a few years and she called to confide in me that she was dealing with alcoholism. Sharon's stepfather was an alcoholic whom she loved but whom she greatly feared when he was drinking, so much so that sometimes she hid in a closet so that he wouldn't find her."

        —Sherrie Jenkins

Although it was everywhere, I couldn't understand cruelty. It simply made no sense. I vividly remember a time when I was roller skating and another girl pushed me, laughing while I was down on the ground. Why did she do this?

I wanted to be accepted by everyone. I knew that God and Jesus loved me. Wanting to be closer to Them, I asked to be baptized when I was seven. In the eyes of my mother and the leaders of our church, though, I was too young.

Almost two years later, I again asked to be baptized. The minister came to our house and we sat together on the front porch talking about why I wanted to do this. After a lengthy discussion, our pastor walked back inside smiling and shaking his head. "That's one very determined young lady," he told my mother. I wouldn't take no for an answer.

On my ninth birthday, dressed in a white gown and with shaking knees, I was immersed. What a thrill! Afterwards, everyone came up to offer their congratulations, making me feel important. "Finally," I thought, "I belong to God's family."

Church continued to be my safe haven, although I received conflicting messages even there. I knew that God loved me, but I was taught that He rewards us when we please Him and punishes us when we evoke His wrath, often through the forces of nature. As I entered puberty and began to experience natural sensations that accompany the transformation from childhood into adolescence, I began to believe that these feelings were sinful. I was certain that God was furious and would strike me down with lightning. Needless to say, I didn't have a fondness for thunderstorms. Thankfully, we didn't get too many in Southern California.

My confidence continued to spiral downward. At home, Mother and I received constant criticism from my stepfather. His drinking escalated, as did the physical abuse. Once he almost pulled all of my hair out. Mother nearly left him over that.

I learned very young to people-please and lie to avoid getting hurt so much. Often, the lies backfired. When I was a third grader, practically every girl in my class had a baton—it was the latest craze. To gain approval from peers (we had just moved and I was the new kid in school) I told my classmates that my stepbrother's girlfriend, a high school majorette, would give them baton lessons. Of course, she never did. I was very unpopular with the girls until about fifth grade, when they finally either forgot or forgave. During that time I became a tomboy, playing basketball and baseball with the boys since they weren't holding a grudge against me.

I also became a great escape artist. Each time Dad—as I began to call my stepfather—drank, I tried to disappear. I hid in my room, in closets, in a laundry bend, or I fled outside. Sometimes I ran away from home, gone for several hours at a time.

Meanwhile, my biological father kept popping in and out of my life, always at school and always a surprise. Each time I saw him, I felt extremely uncomfortable and just wanted to get back to class. We had nothing in common and nothing to talk about. He usually brought a different woman with him, either a new girlfriend or a new wife, and I thought he was just showing me off.

I couldn't forgive him then for leaving Mother and me. I didn't want to see him anymore. I had a new father who, although abusive, was committed to actively taking on the role of my dad.

"At least he doesn't abandon us," I thought.

When I was thirteen, Mother and Dad had a son. I was so proud to have a baby brother! Mother had been working downtown as a beautician, and after the baby arrived Dad built her a salon in front of our home so that she could watch their son while she worked.

My little brother was fun to take care of, although I didn't babysit him very often. My hours were full with school, church, and, after I turned fourteen and a half, work. I had a busy life and he wasn't a big part of it. Sometimes I even regarded him as a pest, especially when he tore up my homework assignments. Funny how the roles had reversed—I became a lot like my older brother, with no time to give to my younger sibling.

Two days after my brother was born, Dad drove up to the house after work and stumbled inside, gasping for air. He told me to get help, so I hurriedly called the police. The officer arrived and summoned paramedics, who ended up staying a long time. At fifty-four, Dad had a heart attack.

The ambulance team wanted to take him to the hospital but he refused—Mother was still there with the baby and Dad didn't want to scare her. Later that day, my stepbrother came home on leave from the Coast Guard. Still shaken by the incident, I hurried to tell him what had happened. To my surprise and resentment, he was indifferent. He quickly got ready for a date and left me alone to take care of my stepfather.

I didn't sleep a wink that night, staying beside Dad to serve him dinner, give him medicine, and mostly make sure he was fine.

"Don't tell your mother what happened today," he said to me. "We don't need to worry her."

I didn't tell her, but she still found out a week later from a neighbor. She and I were afraid for him, afraid that he might die. But, in a strange sense, that heart attack forged a special bond between Dad and me that hadn't existed before.

Both my parents became highly respected members of our community in large part because of their businesses. Mother ran her beauty shop while Dad built up a large electrical contracting firm. I began to work for him as a secretary on evenings and weekends. In the summers, I worked full time with two weeks paid vacation.

On the job I felt useful and important. I was happy to earn enough money to buy my own clothes; even better, being in the world of business made me feel like an adult. My stepbrother soon took charge of contracting crews while I started to run the electrical parts store. In addition to continuing with my secretarial duties, I sold hardware supplies, bought material, and helped wire houses. Working gave me a tremendously satisfying sense of responsibility.

I was also very busy with school. I loved junior high, where my grades were good, friends abounded, and I was immersed in extracurricular activities. As a member of the school orchestra I played the violin and kettle drums in concerts. I also gave piano recitals. Mother had saved enough money to buy me first a piano, then a violin, and she sewed exquisite formal dresses for the performances.

I directed orchestra, sang in the choir, won letters in sports, taught younger kids how to swim through the Red Cross, and got A's and B's in my classes. I was popular

with friends and with boys, perhaps because I laughed easily, I was kind and genuine with everyone, and I was a good
listener. It didn't matter who they were—rich kids, regular
kids, rough kids—I got along with all of them.

Things were going pretty well in my young life. Even
Dad was getting better. During the entire time I was in
junior high he made a conscious effort to stop drinking.
There was no booze in the house, but occasionally he
lapsed and guzzled cough remedies or anything else he
could find with alcohol in it. He also experienced "dry
drunks" where he behaved as though he was under the
influence even though he wasn't drinking.

But overall, it was a relatively peaceful time at home.
Dad didn't get angry as often, and the rest of us relaxed
more. He tried hard, but unfortunately his abstinence from
alcohol was only temporary.

High school was tougher than junior high, but it was fun
too. I participated in swimming, aquatic ballet, and other
afterschool sports. My best friends and I belonged to a very
active church youth group. We were a close-knit bunch,
going to football games, dances, and the beach together. In
my senior year, I was one of only twenty-five who made it
into a dance production class. We became the top dancers
at school, performing to wide acclaim in numerous shows.

To a casual observer, it might have appeared that I had it
all—good grades, musical talent, athletic abilities, and popu-
larity. But inside of me, as well as at home with Dad resum-
ing his drinking, the battle of darkness raged on. On the
outside, I seemed confident and carefree, but a big part

within was still the frightened, insecure little girl of three. My feelings of worthlessness set me up for being used by others. I needed to be dating all the time, to have a boy around to feel important. I always had to identify with somebody else in order to feel good about myself.

Guys, even older men, must have sensed my neediness because they often tried to take advantage of me. I did my best to defend myself. My own dentist leaned over to kiss me during a dental appointment when I was only thirteen. I angrily pushed him away. Later I learned that he too was an alcoholic.

Sometimes I used creative tactics to fend off hormone-driven teenage boys. When I was fifteen, I walked to the park with a boy I was dating. We started smooching, and soon his hand started inching its way up my dress. I said no. He reached over and grabbed my breast.

"I wish I had one of those," he said.

I pushed him away, took out my falsie, threw it at him, and walked straight home, leaving him dumbfounded with a fake breast in his hands. Years later, when we saw each other at our 30-year class reunion, we laughed as we recalled this crazy episode from our youth.

When I was a high school sophomore, a friend introduced me to a young man whom I fell for right away. He was two years older than me, a senior, with jet-black hair and warm brown eyes. We started to date, going to dances, movies, and picnics.

We became serious about each other very quickly, and talked about marriage. He worked at a nursery, and we both dreamed of owning such a place one day. We were deeply in love, but we fought a lot mainly because I refused to give in to his pressures to have sex.

After seven months together, we broke up. My heart broke too. Then one day, from out of the blue, he invited me to go to the movies with him. My hopes soared—maybe he wanted to ask me to be his girlfriend again. I would have said "yes" in an instant! But when the film was over, he told me he was going to marry another girl with whom he had been intimate. I felt totally betrayed. They were wed, and I heard they had a son. I never saw him again.

Not long after receiving the devastating news from my first true love, I went on a trip to see relatives in Arkansas. It was nice to get away. A distant male cousin took me under his wings, bringing me along to enjoy water skiing and other exciting activities.

I was very needy and vulnerable at that point in my life. This man took the time to listen to me when nobody else seemed to. He made me feel beautiful and loved. One thing led to another, and before I knew it I lost my virginity with him. He was thirty-seven, and an alcoholic. I was sixteen.

The shame, guilt, and sorrow I experienced over this act was pervasive. Even today, it hurts so much to know that I did this.

Chapter 4

The End Of Dreams

*With my dreams and aspirations reaching dead ends,
I ran out of options.*

I love to daydream,
      I love to pretend.
My dreams did not become
      A reality at this time.
I will continue dreaming
      And maybe in my lifetime
I will see my dreams
      Well and alive —
Yes, reality of my dreams
      Will survive.
          —Sharon Cook

Every time I watched birds flying through the vast sapphire sky, I was filled with both a sense of freedom and a deep longing. I wanted to soar with them.

As a child I had often dreamed of being a pilot, but in high school I felt this goal was way beyond my reach. The next best thing, in my mind, was to become a flight attendant—a stewardess, as they were called back then.

In the fifties, the job of a stewardess was perceived as glamorous and prestigious. She was paid well, was regarded highly, and traveled. I wanted the chance to see more of our country, to fly, and to make a good living, so I applied for the position with several airlines and anxiously awaited their responses.

I waited, and waited, and waited, but I never received a reply. My dream was slowly dying. Why didn't they write back? Were my grades not good enough? Was I not pretty enough to be a stewardess? What was wrong with me?

Many years later, I learned that the companies had responded favorably and that I met the requirements. Mother had read all the letters which came in, but out of her own fears and insecurities tore them up without telling me. She didn't like the idea of her daughter flitting about on airplanes to unknown, faraway places. Mother also said that she and Dad didn't have the finances to put me through training.

Thinking that I had failed to qualify as a stewardess candidate, I looked elsewhere. Ever since I was a little girl, I loved to dance, to express my creativity through movement and choreography. My high school dance production instructor told her students that we all had the potential to be professional dancers. She motivated us to follow our dreams.

Her encouragement inspired me to send letters to many agents. But once again, I received no replies. Maybe Mother tore those up too, maybe none ever came. I don't know.

I do know that my parents didn't want their daughter to be a professional dancer, either. They thought a dancer's lifestyle would be inappropriate for me. Perhaps to discourage me from following this path, they told me that I wasn't pretty enough to be a dancer. Unfortunately, I came to believe it.

I then decided to attend a Christian college to pursue another lifelong dream: Becoming a missionary. I chose Phillips University in Oklahoma because I heard great things about it from our church youth director, a Phillips graduate and a fine person who became my role model. Sometimes he talked about the South Sea islands, and I began to picture myself as a missionary there. Our church had a college scholarship program which I applied for. I briefly mentioned to Dad my desire to attend Phillips University.

"What do you want to do that for?" he replied. "You're just going to get married, anyway."

Looking back, I realize that my stepfather didn't want me going anywhere because I had become instrumental in his business. I ran the store, my stepbrother ran the electrical contracting side, and we covered for Dad whenever he went on drinking binges. After trying to stay sober for three years, he succumbed to being a periodic alcoholic with some of his sprees lasting for a month at a time. Dad's alcoholism made him dependent on his children; he needed us to keep the business running.

With my dreams and aspirations reaching dead ends, I ran out of options. It seemed that the only future left for me was getting married and having children.

Chapter 5

Destructive Behavior

As young, starry-eyed newlyweds, we were happy and in love, but we entered our marriage with secrets hiding in our hearts.

"Our friendship continued after high school, but we didn't become really close friends until after Sharon married. We did a lot of things together with our children, but probably due to the long hours that our husbands worked we became each other's confidant and usually talked on the telephone almost daily, sometimes more than once a day. Our friendship really helped each other since both of us spent a lot of time alone with only the company of very young children. When it became apparent that Sharon's marriage was in trouble, she confided in me and totally trusted me. I saw her through many difficult times."
—Sherrie Jenkins

After my first true love left me, I was so lonely that I prayed someone else would enter my life. Then I met Allen[1].

He walked by Dad's store almost every day to a little coffee shop two doors down the street. I went inside that shop one afternoon and found him having lunch with a mutual friend. We were introduced, and I was in love. To my delight, Allen was attracted to me, too.

He was a fireman, handsome, worldly, and seven years older than me. He had served in the Korean War as a marine. Overall, he was a quiet man, but he became ani-

---

[1] Assumed name

mated whenever he talked about his passion, cars. To me, Allen's life was infinitely more exciting than mine.

We had coffee together often and spoke of marriage right from the beginning. It wasn't long before Allen and I started going steady, but I left him when I learned he was dating others. Our separation was short-lived, though—he set out to win me back and convinced me that I was the one for him. He spoiled me, buying expensive presents and lavishing me with attention. We started to date again and quickly settled down to a serious relationship, making plans for our future wedding.

Nine months after I graduated from high school with the Class of '58, Allen and I were wed. I was eighteen, he was twenty-five. We were married on a Wednesday to take advantage of his extended off-duty period. Because it was mid-week, we expected only about seventy-five guests. Were we overwhelmed with joy when over one hundred fifty arrived, including the town's entire fire department!

It was the high point of my young life but, like many weddings, it had its share of stress. My dad was moody that evening, keeping me guessing until the last minute as to whether or not he would walk me down the aisle. Thankfully, he did escort me. The rest of the evening unfolded like a dream come true.

Allen and I honeymooned two fabulous days in Palm Springs, then returned to live in a cute little apartment across the street from my parents. It was a good setup; our privacy was respected yet Mother was nearby when I needed her.

As young, starry-eyed newlyweds, we were happy and in love, but we entered our marriage with secrets hiding in our hearts. I couldn't bear to tell my husband that I had already experienced intimacy with another man with whom I had lost my virginity. Allen told me that he had been engaged to a state beauty contest winner who later married one of his friends. I felt she was still dear to him and I secretly feared that I could never measure up to her. An invisible barrier of guilt and resentment began to divide me from my husband.

Throughout his life, Allen always seemed to take on the role of caretaker and provider. His childhood had been a sad, difficult one. When he was five, his father left his mother for another woman. His mother developed ulcers and died, with her son at her bedside when he was only seven.

Afterwards, his grandmother raised him. She was a housekeeper for an elderly man whom he hated, I don't know why. There were many things Allen never shared with me, such as his experiences in Korea and his reasons for despising his grandmother's employer. My husband preferred to keep most of his thoughts to himself, I quickly learned.

Unwittingly, we both brought unresolved issues into our marriage. He carried the hurt from his past, and I had anger raging deep inside. We acted upon our negative feelings in different ways. He neither drank nor smoked, but he became a workaholic, escaping the pain through his jobs. Meanwhile I proceeded to bring chaos into our household, recreating the frenzied mood which permeated my child-hood homes. I picked fights and lashed out for no reason.

Allen took on a second job at a furniture store on his days off, partly so that I wouldn't have to keep working for Dad who fired me again after another of his drinking spells. Dad's alcoholism was getting worse, making him increasingly difficult to be around.

My health was in poor shape. I was 5'5" tall but weighed only 107 pounds. I was anemic, anorexic (although I didn't realize it at the time), had no energy, and experienced frequent, terrible cramping pains in my abdomen. My body was sick, but my soul was ailing even worse. I felt unlovable. I didn't know why, but I hated myself. My self-defacing feelings were leading me down a slow path to destruction.

Still, a brighter side of me resolved to be the best wife and, soon, the best mother I could possibly be. I treasure the memories of our first Christmas together as husband and wife. It was 1959, and we had a beautiful white tree with blue ornaments. Our blessings were many, but the greatest by far was the baby on the way.

In the spring of 1960, we moved from our little apartment into a three-bedroom, two-bathroom house which Dad bought for us to live in. He purchased one for my step-brother as well, who by then was married and had a baby boy. We paid rent and later bought the house from Dad when we could afford to.

Allen was on duty the night in August that I began to have intense labor pains. I drove myself to the hospital, meeting him there. It seemed like we paced up and down the halls forever trying to get our baby to emerge. After a long and arduous labor, David was born. He was a beautiful newborn, and his determination showed up early. David had to wear a cast and later special shoes for many months to correct a foot which was turned in at birth. The cast simply became a part of him, and he learned to walk with it at eleven months.

My husband was away at work so much that Mother hired someone to assist me with the baby. I appreciated the help, especially since David slept little and sometimes had severe seizures. Doctors ruled out epilepsy but didn't know what was bringing on these violent spells which plagued David for several years before they disappeared completely when he was eight.

Since physicians weren't sure how to treat David, I tried everything that anyone suggested to stop the seizures. I spanked him, I threw water at his face, but of course these actions did nothing but add to my growing guilt.

We had dropped out of church for a while, but we started participating again after David came into our lives. Sundays were blissful. We went to Sunday School and socialized with other young married couples. After church, we took lazy drives to a nearby resort community for brunch. We did all the typical family activities and relished our roles as mommy and daddy.

In January of 1962, I became pregnant again. Shortly after receiving the wonderful news at the doctor's office, I got some bad news: Two huge cysts had developed in my ovaries. There was no way to tell if they were cancerous, so surgery for a partial hysterectomy was scheduled for March. The possible effects on the baby were unknown.

Our insurance wouldn't cover the operation, putting a tremendous load on Allen who continued to work long hours at two jobs to support a growing family. I could tell that he was very afraid of losing me to cancer. He was already in a state of emotional vulnerability since his grandmother and a close uncle had recently passed away. The thought of his wife dying next, leaving him with a young boy to raise alone, was something he couldn't face.

I was frightened, too, for myself, for David and Allen, and for the new life growing within me. I prayed, prayed, and prayed with all my heart for the tumors to go away.

Three days before the scheduled surgery, my doctor checked me and was astonished to find that the cysts had vanished. What a relief! A true miracle had taken place.

In September, Allen and I left David with Mother and hurried to the hospital. Labor went by quickly and in just a few hours our second son, Robert, was born. He was a sweet, calm baby.

Our little family was complete, and it was a very happy time for all of us. Dad wasn't drinking quite as much, and I could tell he was feeling compassion for me. I remember that he sent me a gorgeous bouquet of yellow roses shortly before Robert's birth.

Allen left the furniture store and took on a job at a citrus plant. I became very involved with our church and with David's school. I kept busy with our fast-growing boys, taking them to birthday parties and outings. Sometimes we went to the beach with Mother and my young half-brother. I loved to sit on the warm sand and watch the three little boys running and giggling together.

About this time, several former members of my high school dance production class and I decided to join the YWCA to practice dancing together again. With babysitting provided on the premises, we could dance without worrying about our babies. It was a great experience: Our friendships were renewed, and my dream of being a professional dancer materialized to some degree.

I tried out for a production and was elated to be accepted and to have the opportunity to dance in two shows. Unfortunately I couldn't let Allen know about this. He was adamantly opposed to his wife performing, claiming that the stage was no place for a mother.

I loved being a mommy, but I needed something for myself away from home. Allen wouldn't even think of letting me work because he wanted to be the sole financial provider. So I started to volunteer at a hospital while Robert stayed at a daycare center and David went to kindergarten. It satisfied a need I had to serve in a capacity other than housewife and mother.

Even though things seemed to be going well for me, I was still empty inside. My anger would surge unexpectedly, driving me to push Allen into arguments. After each fight, I felt a tremendous sense of relief. I knew this was not normal, but I had no idea what to do about it.

Allen was the recipient of anger coming from all directions. He had gone to work for Dad and enjoyed learning about the electrical contracting business. But my stepfather blew up one day and fired him for no apparent reason, forcing my husband to get another job with a competitor.

About this time, Allen's tragic childhood memories crashed head on with the reality of his adult life where two dysfunctional people were blindly trying to make their marriage work. He sunk into a deep depression and, when not on duty at the fire station, spent most of his time sleeping. His withdrawal from life just fueled my fury even more.

There we were, two mixed-up people attempting to do the right things but drifting apart. I could tell Allen had a crush on a woman he met while working. She was an artist, and we attended one of her shows where I immediately sensed that he felt something for her. At the same time, Allen knew that I had feelings for a man I'd known for years. Our marriage was in trouble.

In 1969, I went to work for a medical laboratory. I felt as though I had just been released from jail. The sense of freedom I had was almost intoxicating. I loved going to work, maybe in part because my home environment was a disappointment to me.

I argued with Allen about everything. He further with-drew into his own silent world. Our boys were sick much of the time, just as I had been as a frightened little girl. They absorbed their parents' pain and anger, suffering quietly. I thought I had escaped my war-zone childhood homes, but all I had done was recreate the scenario with my new family, harming my sons the way I had been hurt. Ever so subtly, I passed the darkness on to my own innocent children.

After ten years of faithfulness to Allen, my infatuation with men took possession of me and I had an affair. My soul was so polluted that instead of feeling guilty, I felt attractive, exciting, and alive. My appetite for attention from men led me to a string of affairs.

I manipulated my husband and lied to him, even though he had begun a sincere attempt to meet my needs. He sometimes picked me up at work so that we could enjoy lunch together. He often watched the children and prepared dinner for the family, making sure it was warm and ready for me at the end of the day. I kept up appearances well, looking like a good wife and a great mother. But behind closed doors, I led a secret, wild life.

I knew I was out of control, and at some level I wanted to get help in order to resolve our issues and repair our lives. I insisted that we see a counselor, and Allen agreed to go. I also read many self-help books, consulted psychics, tried many things to change myself and to salvage our marriage.

During counseling, it became clear that Allen believed I, alone, was wounding our family and only I needed help. I accepted responsibility for my part in our problems, but I wanted him to recognize that he too had unresolved issues which were hurting our relationship. His lack of interest to get help for himself discouraged me.

By then, ten-year-old David was developing a deep resentment towards me. "If Mom wouldn't push Dad so much," he told our counselor, "everything would be OK."

Robert, at the tender age of eight, was a sensitive, intuitive child. He seemed very mature, taking on responsibilities for others and putting upon himself much of the grief emanating from our household. My behavior was hurting him to the core.

I knew I was damaging my husband and our sons, but I felt helpless to alter my lifestyle. Rendezvousing with prominent businessmen made me feel like somebody important. If I couldn't stop seeing them for my children's sake, who or what could make me change?

I abandoned counseling for the wrong reasons. I gave up trying to fix our home life in part because I felt Allen was blaming me for everything and was unwilling to work things out. I continued to lie, stir up fights, cheat on Allen, and cover my tracks.

Meanwhile, my stepbrother was dying of lung cancer. Dad's business was going broke, and soon he and Mother separated because she could no longer tolerate his alcoholism. My whole family was falling apart.

I visited my stepbrother at the hospital and genuinely tried to talk with him, but he didn't want me there. He was bitter, hopeless, and angry at everyone. His wife had left him and remarried, getting her second husband to adopt the three children she had with my stepbrother. He felt completely defeated, with nothing left to live for. After he died, I couldn't bring myself to go to his funeral. I watched it take place across the street through a window at work.

Life went on, and in 1972 I met the owner of a business I sometimes stopped by to look at beautiful antique furniture on display. He started to pursue me, and I let him wine and dine me. Wayne[2] was charming, witty, and brilliant. We went out dancing and to mind-expanding cultural events— activities that Allen and I never did together anymore. My moments with Wayne were sheer ecstasy compared to my monotonous married life.

On Easter Sunday of that year, Robert was baptized. It was supposed to be a special, treasured day for him and for our family, but I ruined it. My deep-rooted anger had built up to an explosive level and, instead of rejoicing at my son's baptism, all I could think of was my mounting desire to leave Allen. After church, I asked my husband to take us out to dinner. He said no, and I blew up. I made a horrible scene and asked him to leave.

Allen started to cry, then left. It was only the second time I had ever seen him weep. The first was when we visited his mother's grave site as newlyweds. I took the boys to Mother and rushed over to see Wayne, telling him that I had ended my marriage.

---

[2] Assumed name

Today, I can't comprehend how I could rip my family apart particularly on what was supposed to be a momentous occasion for my child. I can't bear to think of the consequences my cruelty must have born on Robert's life.

But back then, I felt no remorse. I only felt relief that my mundane life was over, and that I could be with the new man I had fallen in love with. The two weeks after our separation were blissful for me, but they were sheer hell for Allen.

He asked our minister to talk with me. He even was baptized in the hopes that this act would somehow bring me back. I finally told him I was in love with another man. Allen was devastated.

We started divorce proceedings, selling the house and dividing everything up fairly. The boys and I moved into an apartment close to where I worked. Their father paid child support and saw our sons frequently. When he took them on longer trips, I escaped to Las Vegas with Wayne. He was still married, so I saw him whenever he could get away.

Allen and I agreed that David and Robert would benefit from attending a parochial school. It gave our sons the stability which was completely lacking in their home life.

There I was, separated from my husband, alone with two boys, dating a married man, spiritually broken, and—to compound matters even further—on the road to the early stages of alcoholism.

Chapter 6

Repeating Patterns

By the time I reached thirty, I was consuming about three hard liquor drinks a week.

It only takes a moment to say an unkind word,
  Or to pass along gossip you have just overheard.
It only takes a moment to shoot a gun
  Then someone's life is over and done.
It only takes a moment to commit a crime,
  A rape, a murder, a stolen car,
all done at the drop of a dime.
It only takes a moment for a criminal to go free,
  A life of repeated crimes—no rehabilitation
    But they are out on bond to hurt you and me.
It only takes a moment for all to be taken away —
  Jobs, health care, or life savings, all gone in a day.
It only takes a moment to hate someone
because of race.
  A child doesn't know the color of skin
    But instead of a smile there's a frown on his face.
It only takes a moment for alcohol to change
the person you are.
  You feel like you own the world
    Until you kill someone while driving your car.
It only takes a moment to watch what
    a child can do —
  There are lessons we can learn, so let's
start, me and you.
It only takes a moment to help someone every day.
  God is always there to help—it only takes
a moment to pray.
          —Anna Raye Skaggs

Throughout my teenage years, I successfully resisted the
temptation to touch alcohol. I was paranoid about becoming like my stepfather, so I refused to go near it. The first

time I had a drink was when I tried champagne punch at a wedding Allen and I went to as newlyweds.

Four years later, when I was twenty-two, I began to experience problems in the bedroom. As Allen and I lay together, memories of the man who molested me when I was five came flooding back. I felt terribly guilty because I no longer could be intimate with my husband.

I sought advice from my doctor, who suggested that I try drinking a glass of wine beforehand to help me relax. One evening, I took his advice to the extreme. I drank about a dozen screwdrivers before we made love. The next morning, I couldn't remember a thing that had happened the night before, even though my husband said we had a great time.

After that black-out episode I didn't drink again until I was twenty-nine, after I began working at the laboratory and having affairs. At first, I insisted on meeting my lovers at coffee shops, not bars, because I didn't want to be near booze. Ironically, most of the men I dated were, or later became, alcoholics.

But eventually I started to sip wine coolers after work, before Allen came home, to relax. By the time I reached thirty, I was consuming about three hard liquor drinks a week.

After I met Wayne, I went deeper into the stages of alcoholism as we both spiraled down into murkier darkness.

Chapter 7

Into The Pit

It was a new world for me, a crazy, carefree, and excessive one which I jumped into headfirst.

I was a woman in war and my ally was darkness.
  I put my boots of fear on,
I put my uniform of pride and power on.
  I loaded my gun with greed and lust,
I picked up my gun with hate.
  I shot my gun with anger.
The war was being won with my allies:
  Darkness, fear,
    pride, greed, power,
  lust, hate, and anger.
          —Sharon Cook

People say that love can be blind. That certainly was the case for me with Wayne. Had I been seeing straight, I would have run in the opposite direction instead of into his arms.

The Wayne I fell in love with was extraordinary: A genius and a sophisticate loaded with charisma. He worked hard all of his life to reach an elevated social and financial status. A scientist, an inventor, a successful businessman—I was in complete awe of this man and his accomplishments.

On our first formal date, he took me to an elegant restaurant on the waterfront. What a conversationalist! History, jazz, science, law, sports —there wasn't a subject he couldn't handle. He told me I was the first girl he had ever met who could keep up with him intellectually. I should have picked up on his condescending attitude towards women immediately, but I was too busy soaking up the flattery he dished out freely.

He pushed all the right buttons, telling me I was beautiful and treating me like a queen. I was so infatuated with him that I overlooked a major flaw—his anger surfaced quickly and easily. I remember saying to him that there was no need for him to be so short and angry with others, but I didn't think that there was reason for me to be concerned.

Wayne rented an apartment where we could meet, our own romantic hideaway. I felt special to have him get a place just for the two of us.

After I left Allen in 1972, I figured it would be no time at all before Wayne left his wife and married me. To my disappointment, he wasn't ready for such a drastic change. For his convenience, he intended on staying married while we had our affair.

In time, Wayne said he fell deeply in love with me. His divorce was final in 1974, and we were married a month later on a docked ship. We lived it up in San Francisco on a mini-honeymoon, donning chic hats, stylish clothes, and my flawless full-carat diamond ring. Wayne hid it in the potato salad the afternoon he proposed to me on a picnic. He had a sense of humor.

We were a ready-made family with four sons, my David and Bob (as we began to call Robert) and Wayne's two boys. His youngest was six, my oldest was fourteen. Initially I thought he was a great father, playing sports with our sons and communicating well with all four.

My new husband and I sizzled together in a relationship filled with passion. I enjoyed dressing in seductive outfits which he bought for me to wear in the bedroom. We often retreated to our apartment to have complete privacy. It seemed as though we would be newlyweds forever.

We regularly stayed out dancing long past midnight and then hopped to a nightclub where we drank and listened to music until six in the morning. It was a new world for me, a crazy, carefree, and excessive one which I jumped into headfirst.

It was my younger son, Bob, who finally said to me, "Mom, you've really changed."

And I had. Partying, dancing all night, drinking—when did I have time to be the mother my sons needed? I tried to be there for them as well as for Wayne's sons who lived with us four days a week, but I know their needs were not met. I lived for my escapades with Wayne.

We went to Europe a few months after our wedding for our big honeymoon, where we saw thirteen countries in thirty days and drank every night. Wayne was the life of the party wherever we went, telling one joke after another and impressing everyone with his extensive knowledge of European history. He had eyes for all the pretty girls, making me extremely jealous.

When we returned home, the medical lab I worked at—whose practice was to dismiss female employees who were not self-supporting—laid me off because I married a financially stable businessman. My self-esteem took a dive. I liked my job, and I also liked having my own income because it meant I didn't have to be completely dependent on my husband.

Wayne didn't believe that I was let go. He was certain that I quit and always resented me afterwards. He wanted me to be employed. I did too. I started working with him, but we clashed. Soon, I decided it would be wise to spend more time with our sons, which made my husband angry because he thought I was deserting him and the business.

Slowly, I began to see more clearly the angry side of the man I married. His resentment towards his mother surfaced repeatedly, spawning heated arguments between them in full viewing range of customers. He was often extremely rude to her. I didn't understand this behavior.

My sons also began to receive verbal abuse from their stepfather. Bob's sensitive nature made him a prime target. He stood up for his rights and rebelled against his step father, so Wayne ridiculed him often and shamed him to try to break his spirit. David didn't get it as badly because he learned to people-please in order to stay out of trouble.

We took our boys on a trip across the country in 1975, stopping along the way to see my biological father. I was very hurt because my father spent more time with Wayne than with me. I wanted to try developing a relationship with him, but my husband managed to take over the limelight. My sons were disappointed because their grandfather paid more attention to their stepbrothers than to them. It was a difficult trip.

When our vacation was over, Wayne and his parents decided to sell their business. It was a time of transition and great uncertainty for us. My husband took Valium to calm down. I got a job at an escrow company but soon was fired because I couldn't concentrate. I found another job at a doctor's office and Wayne obtained a realtor's license. While he sold properties, I quit my position in order to care for our sons. Soon I became a realtor and he quit sales to return to work as a scientist. We were restless and just didn't seem to know what to do with our lives.

Through it all, we kept drinking, partying, and fighting. One night, my husband physically abused me while the boys huddled together in fear. Another time, he physically abused Bob in our garage. I was too drunk to rescue my own son. Since I did nothing to stop Wayne from hurting my son, I became a co-abuser. It was no surprise when Bob started drinking at the age of fifteen.

My mother didn't like to visit us anymore. "Your home feels evil," she would grieve.

She was right. Tremendous darkness had taken over our lives.

Chapter 8

Crawling Out

*She asked, "Have you been drinking?" I denied it.
Frustrated, she said, "You need a spiritual awakening."*

The first time I met Sharon was at a recovery meeting in 1983. I remember thinking she looked very pale and sad. As soon as we started to talk I knew we would be friends. I had no idea how close we would really be. Through a series of meetings she was finally convinced to go into treatment for her alcoholism.

Being new to sobriety myself, all that I knew how to do was stay with her and take her to meetings. I was worn out! When she went to the hospital I remember telling her she needed a spiritual awakening. Little did I know what was to happen in the future.

She returned spouting all these revelations she had learned in treatment. I was furious, since I had been drumming these same things into her head for weeks. Well, she took off like a cannon shot. She dragged me to everything she could think of having to do with sobriety. What a lesson for me. All I had to do was mention something I wanted to do and guess what? She had all the information and we were off doing it.

Thank God for Sharon, because I don't believe I would have learned what I know today if she had not dragged me along. The experience gave us both a life of our own, something we had never had before. Sharon's husband began to dislike me for taking her away and giving her all these new ideas. I know he blames me for the problems they had. He just didn't understand that she was growing without him. As she became more her own person, he became more of a controller.

I moved away, but we stayed in touch with each other. One day I received a call from Sharon that we needed to renew our friendship, which had become strained. I had watched her being victimized by her husband on a regular basis and it was very hard for me to deal with.
	—Judy Gentry

It got to the point that Wayne and I drank heavily at home every night in addition to consuming large amounts of alcohol each time we went out to weekday happy hours or weekend bashes.

I was on my way to pick up Bob at his job one evening when, being completely intoxicated, I ran into a parked car. Bob got a ride from a friend while David located me and took me home. I paid for damages to the other car and was fortunate to stay out of jail, thanks to David, whose friendship with local police officers kept them from pressing charges against me for driving under the influence.

Another night, Wayne and I went out drinking. As I always did on our dates, I wore a slinky, seductive outfit. And, as often was the case, we fought. He became furious and stormed out, leaving me alone at the bar. I walked to my car in the parking lot and started to drive away. I didn't get very far when a gang of teenagers jumped into my car and kidnapped me. Police stopped them, but the ruffians said they were just riding with me. I was too drunk and frozen with fear to try to escape or cry out for help. The officers left, and we drove to an empty field. After several agonizing moments during which I didn't know what was going to happen, they took my wallet and fled on foot. I was thankful to be left unharmed.

I drove home where I found Wayne drinking. Sobbing, I told him of my ordeal. "Well, you deserved it," was his reply.

Our private bedroom moments grew more and more bizarre. Wayne wanted me to be a domineering partner. I obliged even though I had to be drunk to participate. He also wanted to swap partners, but I refused. Instead, he became obsessed by adult book material and I had a secret affair. I sought a lover who would protect me and be my caregiver. I felt my sex life with him was more normal—if having an affair can be called normal.

In 1978, I was physically abused again by my husband. My face, arms, and legs were black and blue. When Bob saw me later that day, his eyes reflected intense hatred. Both my sons and I spent the night with my half-brother and his wife. The next day the boys went to work and I stayed at a motel. When I returned home, my husband was ready with an expensive ring and profuse apologies. I stayed.

Hard to imagine, but our alcoholism worsened. It seemed as though alcoholism and abuse went hand in hand in our family. At the same time, Bob turned wild and became completely dependent on cocaine while David went out with many girls in a desperate search for love.

In 1981, violence emerged in our bedroom again. Bob came to my rescue, but his stepfather turned on him. My son ran out of the house to save his life and stayed with a friend that night. The next day, he rented an apartment and left home for good. David remained with us to keep an eye on me, always sleeping with a baseball bat under his bed just in case.

By now Wayne's youngest son was thirteen and plagued by arthritis. Shortly after the diagnosis his bowels ruptured and he was rushed to emergency, barely surviving.

Wayne and I were given permanent custody of his sons and I became their full-time caretaker. At first I was resentful because my husband had driven my own son, Bob, away from home. But soon I softened and accepted the responsibility of parenting his boys, loving them as my own.

For the next year and a half, my life consisted of shuttling our youngest to schools, doctors, and counselors. There was tremendous anger raging inside of him as a result of his illness and because of living with alcoholic parents. Once, Wayne was so intoxicated that he also physically abused his young son, adding to his pain and indignation. Again, I was too full of alcohol to intervene. And again, I was a co-abuser.

His older brother fell into a deep depression and slept all day long when he wasn't attending college classes. I saw David and Bob very little during that period, even though my oldest still lived with us. David continued to date many girls, looking for love and becoming addicted to relationships. Bob remained hooked on cocaine until he awoke one morning bleeding heavily from his nose. He then switched to marijuana.

Life remained the same as time marched on, each of us broken, each with addictions and agonized states of mind. Wayne and I continued our destructive behavior. David would call the police whenever violence erupted, but when they arrived I would never press charges. Once Wayne hit David after he came to my defense. After that, my oldest son—who had remained with us to protect me—left to live on his own.

Sometimes, I took long drives by myself to escape. I had become desperately lonely, so much so that I even made up phony surveys just to go door to door and talk to strangers. When Wayne's sons visited their mother, I disappeared into a motel to drink, sometimes with my husband and other times alone.

In 1983, a miracle started to take place. Wayne and I realized our drinking was out of control and we talked about stopping. We tried, managing to stay sober for three days at a time. We were supportive of each other in our new mission, but we kept slipping back to drinking.

David's girlfriend sent me something about a recovery program for alcoholics. I called the number in the brochure, and the woman who answered patiently talked with me for a long time. She told me about a meeting that was scheduled for that very evening. I phoned Wayne and asked if he would come with me to the meeting. He said yes!

At that first gathering I met Judy, a very special person who became one of my closest friends. We went out for coffee the next day and talked. Thereafter Judy contacted me daily, and we went to meetings every night. I stayed away from alcohol for two weeks. Then I woke up depressed one morning and, after looking at our family with its assortment of problems, I resorted to drinking to numb the pain.

That morning I was scheduled to meet Judy at her house. When I arrived, she asked, "Have you been drinking?" I denied it. Frustrated, she said, "You need a spiritual awakening."

I had promised Bob that if the self-help meetings didn't work, I would go into treatment. Judy thought the time had come. She called my husband and they took me to a drug and alcohol treatment center. I was in detox for twenty-four hours and have been sober since, from July 26, 1983, to the present. Thirteen years so far, with the help of God.

I thought I was to remain in treatment just a few more days, but I had to stay the full twenty-eight days of the program in order for our insurance to cover the cost. At first I was furious. Then it hit me: I had been crying out to God for help for so many years, and here it was.

This was my turning point. Committed to staying sober, I threw myself totally into the program.

Wayne, who was sober thirty days longer than me, came to the hospital every day after work to join me in my classes. We both learned so much. As I reached the end of the program, Wayne enrolled in it. We spent four days in the center together, the first husband and wife team in the program. When I was done, he had three weeks left to go.

After treatment, my hopes were high. I believed things would finally be right with our family. My husband and I continued to attend self-help meetings throughout 1983-1987 while we worked on improving our relationship. During this time I bonded with Wayne's youngest, who became my treasured child. I was finally able to empathize with him and feel his physical, mental, and emotional pain in my heart. I came to love him so much. I went in with him to provide moral support during a surgery. He seemed to rely on me greatly.

In 1985, a reunion was held for those of us who had been in treatment together. Only three out of thirty-five had remained completely sober. In the fall of that year, Judy and I took a giant leap—we enrolled in college to become drug and alcohol counselors.

Wayne and I took up traveling again, this time sober, and toured New Zealand and Australia. On another trip a few years later, we visited Indonesia, Singapore, Bangkok, and Hong Kong. I certainly got to see the world with my second husband.

In 1986, David was wed. Perhaps I should have been happy for him, but I wasn't. I worried that he would repeat the same patterns set by Allen and me in our marriage.

I truly believed that Wayne's and my sobriety would solve many of our problems. But the reality was that our sons were still in dire need of treatment, and our relationship was in jeopardy. Although my husband no longer drank, his anger still surfaced unexpectedly. He continued to put me down, ridiculing my college work. He would not allow me to display my counseling books alongside his science text-books on our shelf. He also controlled me financially.

Through school, I learned about family dysfunction, alco-holism, anorexia, overeating, sexual dependency, and many other addictions plaguing humankind. It was a form of ther-apy for me. I also learned just how sick our own family was.

Even though we were seeing a counselor to help us save our marriage, Wayne remained hooked on adult book mate-rial and I continued with my affair. The counselor told me I had to leave my lover before I could begin to resolve my marriage issues, and I did. Thus I was impelled to look head-on at my troubled relationship with Wayne, without the escape that alcohol or an affair offered.

It began to sink in that our situation was not going to improve. Wayne was capable of treating me like a goddess one minute and like trash the next. He wasn't drinking, but he still failed to respect me and couldn't curb his rage.

I knew I had to do something after having a particularly haunting nightmare. In my sleep I saw a corpse lying inside an oven in our bedroom. I knew I had to get out.

Chapter 9

Divine Intervention

I drove up to the mountains, got out of my car, and screamed with all my might, "God, God! Help me!"

Then the day came when she told me she was leaving Wayne. I was very happy that she had become strong enough to take such a giant step. She lived with me for a while, but was not doing too well on her own. I believe there was still too much anger and fear remaining. She had been so belittled and ridiculed by her husband that she had to go back and find out that it wasn't she who had the problem. In order to survive this time she had to gain strength that came from another source besides herself. I truly believe that God intervened in her life with a true spiritual awakening.

Some of the experiences she shared with me have led me to believe that they were of a supernatural origin. Sharon has always been one of the most honest people I have ever met and not given to delusional thinking. I have seen these experiences transform her from a fearful and indecisive person to an exceptionally insightful and dynamic personality. Today she is doing things that were at one time impossible for me to believe she would ever do, much less on a daily basis. Sharon exhibits love and concern and self-appreciation like most people I know would love to have, including myself. If anyone had known her the way I do and seen this life change they would be profoundly amazed that it is the same person. I love Sharon very much.
    —Judy Gentry

In my first marriage, I was the angry one who lashed out verbally at my spouse. I met my match with Wayne, unwittingly ending up with someone even angrier than me. As long as I remained with him, my own healing could not proceed.

Still, it was hard for me to move on. I wanted very much to remain with my husband and work on developing a new, healthy relationship between us despite every sign I received to leave him.

After being sober for four years, I lay in bed sleeping next to Wayne one night in 1987 when I awoke breathing heavily. My body was scorching hot, and I started to hyperventilate. Suddenly, I felt propelled upwards, then released. I floated up to the ceiling. There was no fear, only a sense of wonder and tremendous freedom. I played with the ceiling like a child with a new toy, watching with amusement as my hands passed through it. I inched a bit higher and continued to put my hands through the surface effortlessly over and over again. It was enthralling. I felt incredibly free.

Then I rolled over and saw my husband laying next to my own body on the bed below. Seeing myself down there frightened me, causing my spirit to reunite with my body instantly.

Why did I have an out-of-body experience? How did it happen? Did I die for a moment? I'm not sure, but I believe I died at some level, perhaps as a result of tremendous emotional pain I was enduring at that time. A part of me wanted to leave Earth and all of my problems behind.

When I returned to my body, I was transformed. Every single cell was alive, jumping, tingling. Electricity was sparking within me. It felt wonderful!

This electric feeling remained with me all night. When it passed, I was disappointed. For a week afterwards, I was angry—I wanted to leave this world for good and feel completely unconfined. But I soon realized it was not yet my time to go. I had many things left to do in this life.

I am no longer afraid of death. It is merely a separation of the spirit from the body. Soon after my experience, I told a good friend what had happened and she believed it was real. I also told my marriage counselor, who was glad that it had been a positive event for me.

I felt blessed. God showed me that there is more beyond this life. Being out of my body took away much of my fear, replacing it with comfort and greater inner strength.

I began to make plans to leave Wayne without his knowledge. I was concerned for my well-being. With help from my mother, I made sure my sons were safe, independent, and financially stable. I didn't want them hurt in any way after I left.

In May of 1988, I went to my mother's home. I lived there and also with Judy for a while until I got my own apartment in the Palm Springs area. I was re-trained in real estate, and Judy and I began to volunteer at a treatment center.

Emotionally, I had shut myself down to be able to leave Wayne. My feelings were buried so deeply inside that I couldn't even cry over the fight against cancer that Judy's husband was struggling with. He and Judy had listened to me patiently late into the night many times, supporting me in my first years of sobriety. Now he was dying, and I felt nothing. I knew I had hit rock bottom.

I drove up to the mountains, got out of my car, and screamed with all my might, "God, God! Help me!"

Back at my apartment that night, I listened to soft, soothing music. Slowly, I began to cry and to feel again. I started pacing back and forth, back and forth in my dwelling as my life passed before my eyes.

In my review, I saw what I had done all these years, particularly to my children and stepchildren. I saw myself in every phase of my life—having affairs, neglecting my sons, becoming an alcoholic, hurting others in so many ways and ultimately hurting myself. I also sensed intuitively that generations of pain had been passed down to me.

The terrible physical pain I had experienced from abuse paled compared to the pain I now felt as I realized what kind of a life I had chosen to live. I must have paced in my small apartment for five or six hours. My heart felt as though it was ripping out of my body over and over again as I replayed what I had done. The pain was horrible.

I had used men and allowed them to use me. My alcoholism hurt myself and others around me. I put husbands and lovers before my sons, who needed me so much. I acted as co-abuser of my four sons. My innocent children, these precious gifts God had put in my care. What had I done to them? I wanted so badly to go back, to start over, to experience each special moment with them again as the loving, nurturing mother I should have been. They deserved so much more than I gave.

As I relived each moment of my life, I cried out from my heart how truly sorry I was. Remorse, regret, and repentance filled my whole being. "I'm sorry, I am so sorry," I prayed. "Please, God, I ask for forgiveness."

Finally, emotionally and physically exhausted after several hours of grieving over my past, I lay down to rest and closed my eyes. Suddenly, a white light filled my room. I opened my eyes, but it glowed so brightly that I had to shut them again. I was afraid its intensity would blind me. It was present for a good minute, then faded away. I stood up and looked out my window. Nobody was around. It was pitch black outside. I lay back down to reflect upon the light.

When I had first felt its presence, I was fearful. But then I felt peace, comfort, and love as I had never known before. I realized this light must have a divine source.

"Why me?" I wondered. Then I understood I was loved and forgiven. Christ's Light had come to take away my pain and to comfort me. How humbled I was. What peace I felt for the first time in my life.

My body and mind were severely wounded.
My soul was full of darkness.
With Christ's Light I was carried away from the war,
And given a Divine Gift of Christ's White Light.
Thank you, God.
        —Sharon Cook

Chapter 10

A Cleansing Within

My experiences helped me to understand the Bible references to light, love, looking within, and receiving the kingdom of God like a little child.

Create in me a pure heart, O God,
And renew a steadfast spirit within me.
Do not cast me from your presence
Or take your Holy Spirit from me.
Restore to me the joy of your salvation
And grant me a willing spirit, to sustain me.
—Psalm 51, Verses 10-12

After God reached out to me with such power, I could no longer turn my back to Him. I knew I was forgiven and that each of our lives has such tremendous purpose. I embarked on a journey to find mine.

Even though I was sober, I had a long way to go to make things right in my life. Temptations still abounded, as they have a tendency to do in life, and I still made many mistakes.

One was returning to Wayne. I believed that after being blessed with sacred out-of-body and White Light experiences, I had the inner strength to make our marriage work.

We began to date and, at first, everything was wonderful all over again. I made plans to move back. Judy clearly saw this as a setback. "I hope you will be very happy," she told me, "but I never before realized just how abused you've been. I wish you well, but I cannot watch you being hurt anymore." And with these parting words, my dear friend left my life for a while.

I moved in with Wayne in October of 1988. My sons were extremely disappointed and downright furious with me for returning to my spouse.

We reaffirmed our marriage vows at church. It was just the two of us and the minister, no family, guests, or witnesses present. Then my husband and I flew to Hawaii for another honeymoon and a fresh new start.

While on the island of Kauai, I had another startling experience. Wayne was sleeping in bed next to me while I lay awake thinking. A vision suddenly appeared before my eyes, and a deep, authoritative voice said, "I am the God of Abraham, Isaac, and Jacob, and I will take care of you through this next year."

I was stunned. "Why?" went through my mind. I thought everything was going great: I was sober, happy, and back with my husband who was willing with me to try again. What was God going to protect me from this next year? I was very naive.

The newlywed bliss lasted for a month, then my eyes were opened and I began to see our family differently. I watched the drama unfold as if I were viewing a movie. Regret filled me as Wayne began to control me again, primarily through money. My heart broke watching our sons continue to be plagued by illnesses and addictions. As our situation worsened, I held on to the voice I heard in Kauai.

After being back in the relationship, I could feel myself losing my physical, emotional and spiritual strengths. I had never stopped going to self-help meetings, but I needed additional support.

I began working again with a therapist to strengthen myself without telling Wayne. I had learned from my past that he used the truths I told him against me in subtle ways. I became a little wiser and protected myself against being further controlled. I didn't like to be dishonest with him, but I had to in order to survive.

Both of my sons started working with me in therapy sessions. It was a great healing process for David and me. Bob and I began to clear away the past, too.

I didn't know it, but another divine intervention was about to occur. As I sat alone in our home one afternoon, resting my weary eyes, I was completely unprepared for what was to happen next. A strong burst of energy shot up the right side of my spine, leaving a hot, burning sensation in its path. When it reached my brain, I saw a kaleidoscope of colors pulsating in my mind. Then the energy raced down my left side, leaving behind an uncanny chill as it passed. I shook fiercely for several seconds after it was over.

"What hit me?" I wondered, completely puzzled and very, very frightened. By then I was six years sober, without a trace of alcohol in my system to affect me in such a bizarre fashion. I thought I might be going crazy.

I began to investigate this latest phenomenon which shook the core of my being. I called a woman I highly respected who was in her fortieth year of sobriety. She suggested that I seek out books describing the Kundalini awakening. I stumbled across a text, through which I learned that we have energy centers in the body. I read about how an energy potential can build up inside a person, particularly someone in a "spiritual emergency," and then suddenly be released either through deep meditation or, as in my case, spontaneously. I learned that my experience was the beginning of a cleansing process.

To this day I don't fully comprehend it, but I think that I had gotten myself so deep into the darkness and that so much anger, hate, and hurt were suppressed inside that this frenzied energy release was necessary for my spiritual cleansing. The words "baptized by fire" come to mind as I reflect on this experience.

The week after my awakening, I felt a purification taking place inside which is hard to describe. The energy pulsating inside my body was difficult to endure. I believe I was being cleansed from my affairs and from the molestation which took place when I was five. I could no longer stand to be intimate with Wayne, or to even be touched by him. At the same time, I began to feel a oneness with God's creation along with true joy emanating from deep within. As I gazed at stars, I knew that I was a little part of what they were made of.

Through this latest divine experience, I learned firsthand of the awesome God-given power and energy that lies in each and everyone of us. To this day I am humbled as I reflect on this.

I sought numerous books and references to learn about myself. I read more about spiritual emergencies and Kundalini awakenings. I also was driven to read the Bible again. This time, its words were clearer to me than ever before. My experiences helped me to understand the references to light, love, looking within, and receiving the kingdom of God like a little child. Several verses in particular made an especially strong impact on me.

In the Old Testament, I read that the prophet Isaiah referred to light as he foretold Christ's birth:

> *The people walking in darkness have*
> *seen a great light;*
> *on those living in the land of darkness*
> *a light has dawned.*
> —Isaiah 9:2

In the New Testament, Jesus is quoted as speaking of light:

> *This is the verdict: Light has come*
> *into the world, but men loved dark-*
> *ness instead of light because their*
> *deeds were evil. Everyone who does*
> *evil hates the light, and will not come*
> *into the light for fear that his deeds*
> *will be exposed. But whoever lives by*
> *the truth comes into the light, so that*
> *it may be seen plainly that what he*
> *has done has been done through God.*
> —John 3:19-21

I learned that light and love go hand in hand. The truth is in light, and love emanates from light. When asked which is the greatest commandment, or the most important of all laws, Christ replied:

> *Love the Lord your God with all your
> heart and with all your soul and with
> all your mind and with all your
> strength. The second is this: Love
> your neighbor as yourself. There is no
> commandment greater than these.*
> —Mark 12:30-31

What comes from the heart—love for God, love for self, love for mankind—is greater than anything else in the universe. To me, someone whose heart is closed is really not alive in the spiritual sense:

> *See to it, brothers, that none of you
> has a sinful, unbelieving heart that
> turns away from the living God. But
> encourage one another daily, as long
> as it is called Today, so that none of
> you may be hardened by sin's deceit-
> fulness.*
> —Hebrews 3:12-13

> *This is the message we have heard*
> *from him and declare to you: God is*
> *light; in him there is no darkness at*
> *all.*
>   —1 John 1:5

> *Yet I am writing you a new command;*
> *its truth is seen in him and you,*
> *because the darkness is passing and*
> *the true light is already shining.*
> *Anyone who claims to be in the light*
> *but hates his brother is still in the*
> *darkness. Whoever loves his brother*
> *lives in the light, and there is nothing*
> *in him to make him stumble. But*
> *whoever hates his brother is in the*
> *darkness and walks around in the*
> *darkness; he does not know where he*
> *is going, because the darkness has*
> *blinded him.*
>   —1 John 2:8–11

I came to realize that our thoughts and actions affect others more than we know. There is a oneness uniting us all:

> *Then make my joy complete by being*
> *like-minded, having the same love,*
> *being one in spirit and purpose. Do*
> *nothing out of selfish ambition or vain*
> *conceit, but in humility consider oth-*
> *ers better than yourselves. Each of*

*you should look not only to your own
interests, but also to the interests of
others.*
  —Philippians 2:2-4

We have the God-given power to live joyfully and to influence others positively. We are responsible for each other. When we hurt someone else, we hurt ourselves. When we help another, we grow. We can make a difference in our lives and in the lives of others, but it must always first start *inside* each of us:

> *Once, having been asked by the
> Pharisees when the kingdom of God
> would come, Jesus replied, "The king-
> dom of God does not come with your
> careful observation, nor will people
> say, 'Here it is,' or 'There it is,' because
> the kingdom of God is within you."*
>   —Luke 17:20-21

Chapter 11

New Beginnings

I was NOT looking for another relationship. But as soon as my gaze rested upon his gentle face, I sensed an instant bond.

Oh my God, how great Thou art!
*   You have truly saved my heart.*
As I look back and see my life,
*   There has been so much strife.*
You constantly intervene to bring me
*   Wisdom and knowledge of Thee.*
Teach me what I must learn
*   To be a servant of the laws of Thee.*
—Sharon Cook

Just as God promised, He took care of me the entire year through demanding and sometimes frightening times. Then in February of 1990, I knew I had to move on. After being with Wayne for sixteen years, I finally accepted that he and I were not right for each other. I left for good, again in secret.

I lived with my mother and worked in real estate. I slowly learned to stand on my own two feet emotionally, physically, and spiritually. It wasn't easy—I had to work hard and cooperate with God to restore myself. The saying, "God helps those who help themselves," was certainly true for me.

Divine intervention moved me away from self-destruction. But it seemed that the darkness continued to try pulling me back to harmful behavior. This time I realized that the light is always working to guide us in the right direction. I was guided towards therapy and self-help groups, which provided me with the support I needed, and to stay-ing sober, which was critical to my whole well-being.

I was very fortunate that Wayne accepted my departure to a sufficient degree. Yes, there were hard feelings; he wasn't happy to see his wife leave. On the few occasions that we came into contact, he subtly tried to intimidate me through mind games. But he did not threaten, monitor, or stalk me. I am thankful that he left me alone.

And alone I was, except for the company of God, my mother, and Judy who came back into my life. Her hus-band had died a year earlier and she was now recently engaged. She dragged me out with her to do things and see people even though I wasn't in the mood to be sociable yet.

I was free and felt as though a burden had been lifted. I was relieved that I didn't have to lie anymore to protect myself. Even though my future was uncertain, I slowly learned to trust that things would be fine. And even though I came to expect dramatic signs from God, I began to understand intuitively that I no longer needed more super-natural experiences to help me along. These were neces-sary to put me back on the right track, but I had reached the point where I could listen to the still, small voice in my heart for guidance.

One glorious afternoon, a girlfriend of mine and I joined Judy at the swimming pool in the resort mobile home park her fiancé lived in. As we lay on beach chairs soaking up the sun and talking, I noticed a very handsome man relax-ing in the pool. I was NOT looking for another relationship.

But as soon as my gaze rested upon his gentle face, I sensed an instant bond.

My friends and I waded into the pool, and the stranger struck up a conversation with us. He looked like a movie star and was friendly with us, clearly enjoying our company. Underneath his broad smile and cool exterior, though, I detected a sad, lonely "little boy."

As he spoke, I could tell he had been drinking heavily. All of my training in alcohol counseling told me not to get involved with someone who has a drinking problem. Yet this man, Larry, had a certain softness and kindness about him which made me feel safe with him. We began to date and have been together ever since.

I would love to say that my relationship with Larry has been a breeze, but that's simply not true. We were on a long and rocky road before becoming the loving, nurturing couple we are today. But it was worth it. Both of us have grown and healed tremendously over the last six years. Love, trust, and commitment saw us through many trying times.

I'll let Larry tell you a bit about our roller coaster ride together:

I met Sharon about six years ago. The part she played as a loving human being was the pivotal point in the reconditioning of my soul. Let me back up and tell you what happened in my life right before Sharon and I met.

After thirty years of marriage, my wife and I had separated—she was living in our home and I was in an apartment. I believed this would be a temporary situation and that everything would return to normal once she came to her senses.

I was a full-blown alcoholic and had just received my first D.U.I. in the state of Washington. My wife called me around this time to tell me she had filed for a divorce complete with restraining orders.

I still didn't believe this was happening. One morning, I awoke way before dawn and drove to the business that my wife and I owned. I intended to work on the accounting books, but I started drinking and decided several hours later to see my wife in order to get this whole thing straightened out. On the way over, I crashed my pickup. The accident destroyed my truck and left me immobilized for several months, and I got a second D.U.I. while still on probation for the first offense.

I received legal documents stating that I was now restrained from going to our business. My wife converted all of our accounts to be in her name only. She also changed the locks on the business. For the first time in my adult life, I was broke.

I lost my driver's license, means of transportation, and income. I was temporarily disabled as I slowly recovered from serious injuries. I lived in an apartment with no furniture. I was lonely, broke, desperate, and scared. And I still refused to believe that my wife would go through with a divorce. My attorney got fed up and fired me as a client because I wouldn't fight against her.

It became a humiliating struggle just to survive. I had to beg my soon-to-be ex-wife for everything from food to rent to taking me to the doctor. Out of desperation, I made a collect call to my parents whom I had ignored for about twenty-five years. They invited me to live with them in their resort mobile home park in Palm Springs until I could get back on my own two feet. I am thankful for this chance they graciously gave me.

While I lived with them, I took a job as a janitor. I thought that if I could prove to my ex-wife that I really could hold down a job she would take me back. It didn't work. Divorce proceedings moved right along.

Finally, something my ex and I owned sold, providing me with enough money to buy my own mobile home in the park my folks lived in. This time I bought a bed, a TV, and a few kitchen items. I received a steady income for a while from the property which had sold. But I did little more than lay drunk in the sun by the pool and drink every morning when I got up. I also drank every time I awoke in the middle of the night so that I could go back to sleep.

I was so lonesome. I felt ashamed of my life and I didn't know what to do about myself or my future. At forty-nine, I really was a scared little boy.

I was drunk in the pool one afternoon when I saw three women approaching. I sat on the steps in the water and waited for the opportunity to talk. When they were close, I overheard them asking each other what the pool hours were. Alas, my chance!

After the small talk, Sharon and I wandered off to a warmer spot. I didn't know it then, but it was natural for her to start talking about recovery. Of course, I played coy and asked all kinds of dumb questions about people who couldn't control their drinking, pretending I was not one of them. I thought I was fooling her the way I thought I fooled everyone else, but the only one who was fooled was me. Sharon knew I was drunk. Still, she stayed with me and we talked for a couple of hours.

To my surprise and delight, she returned to the pool the following day and we resumed our conversation. I learned that Sharon was going through a divorce. Meanwhile my divorce was near completion. We began to date, and my life hasn't been the same since.

Here is where we stood when we first met: I was a total alcoholic while Sharon had been sober for seven years. I was at the tail end of my divorce but still had delusions that my ex and I would get back together. Sharon was certain that she would never return to her ex-husband. I was an atheist. Sharon was spiritually strong. I was immoral, she was moral. I was dishonest, a liar, a cheat; she was completely the opposite. I was a taker, she was a caregiver. With all this in mind, the most remarkable thing about our relationship is that we even began one!

With Sharon's help, I started going to self-help meetings. During this period, I tried to stay sober but failed again and again. I couldn't stay sober for extended lengths of time. The inner pain would become so great that I would cave in. I picked fights with Sharon just to have an excuse to drink. When I could stay sober, we had wonderful times together. When I couldn't, it was a living hell.

Meanwhile Sharon never gave up on me. She nursed me back to mental, emotional, and physical health. She pumped healthy food into me and never stopped talking about recovery!

Even with all that she was doing for me, it still took a year before I fully trusted her. I completely lacked faith in myself and in other people, but Sharon selflessly helped in my restoration.

Sharon is the only person I've ever known who is honest with everyone. She has compassion for people—all people. I admire her greatly. Somewhere in our first year together, I fell in love with that soul inside of Sharon.

Still, the pain that haunted me from my past became too great to tolerate sober. As I proceeded to get drunk yet again, Sharon decided to take drastic measures to stop me from continuing to destroy myself. She hauled me off to a detox center. I was scared and, for the first time in a long, long time I finally acknowledged God, praying to Him for help. I started a recovery program once more, taking it very seriously. Sometimes I attended three meetings a day.

Within the first weeks, I realized that I was setting myself up for the same falls I had taken before. "12 Steps" has a saying that if you can't get honest with yourself you won't stay sober. So I started to take a long, frank look at myself—who I really was and what my problems truly were.

I decided that I should see a therapist. Thank God! At last I got the help I needed.

Our first years together were hard on Sharon. But I was finally coming back to life. My emotions were up and down continuously as different things would make me happy or sad or mad. I began to "feel" again. I could cry once more. I started to see just how fortunate I was. I could tell myself, "I am special. God loves me. Sharon loves me. I'm OK."

Sharon supported me emotionally, physically, and spiritually all these years. She gave me unconditional love. She even drove me around for two years when I didn't have a license.

Had I known before starting this relationship of the pain, the work, the fear of staying sober, had I known I would have to learn about me, had I known I would have to change everything in my life, had I known I would love Christ and develop a relationship with Him, had I known all this I would never have had the courage to start. I'm sure God knows this. I probably would

*have drank myself to death because it was the only way
I knew out of my pain.*

    *I was too weak a person to turn my life around by
myself. I just didn't care and didn't have a reason to
care. God put Sharon in my life to serve up to me a plat-
ter of spiritual example. God served up for me what it
took to save a lost soul, one step at a time.*
                —Larry

Chapter 12

Lending A Helping Hand

It was heart-warming to see these women whose lives had been ruled by alcohol and drug abuse now behaving like little children thoroughly enjoying themselves on Christmas morning.

I had voluntarily gone to treatment for a drug problem. I was writing illegal prescriptions and taking the chance of going to jail. I knew I was defeated—no matter what the consequences, I couldn't stop. Suicide seemed like a viable option. Even if I got out, my husband said he'd take the children from me.

That's where Sharon came in. I was sitting on my bed in treatment and she appeared in the doorway. Her gentleness and love permeated the room. I immediately felt safe.

My concern was for my own children. "What about my children?" I asked again and again. Sharon's reply was, "The only thing you can do for your children is to take care of yourself."

With Sharon's help, I learned how to do that. She became my friend and still is today. She taught me how to love God, myself, and others. She provided a safe environment in which I could work to re-establish my relationship with God, clean up my side of the street and grow in the light that my God has entrusted to me. Today, Sharon is my friend and confidant and always my spiritual advisor. She and the other women whom she introduced me to, including Judy, loved me until I could love myself.

—Fran

When Judy and I were taking classes on drug and alcohol counseling, we dreamed of opening a sober living house. It would be a refuge for recovering alcoholics, a place where they could heal before fully re-entering society as sober individuals.

Our dream came true with help from Larry. Using money that he received from the sale of his business, he purchased a 2,500-square-foot home that had been on the market for a while. It stood by itself with no neighbors nearby—the perfect setting for a sober living house.

A local resort hotel was liquidating its older furniture in preparation for remodeling, so Larry purchased what had been in four of the resort's condominiums. By now, he was seriously working on his recovery and had been sober for nearly a year. He recruited help from several other recovering men to move the furniture into the house. I had fun decorating the place, creating a welcoming, "homey" atmosphere.

We met with a woman in charge of licensing treatment centers in our area. She helped us to develop house rules and criteria appropriate for a sober living environment.

Before we knew it, the special day arrived on August 1st, 1991, when we opened the doors of Triangle House, a sober living home for women. Six ladies ranging in ages from twenty to fifty-three chose to transition back into society here, benefiting from the support this environment offered.

Four women shared two bedrooms and the other two each had their own room. We converted a fifth bedroom into a quiet reading and meditation room. The women were allowed to remain at Triangle House up to a year.

It was quite a learning experience for everyone. I was happy to be able to apply my training in drug and alcohol counseling to such a positive, important project. Through running the sober living home, Larry and I grew and gained a new awareness. Helping these women to recover was richly rewarding.

The house residents learned so much from each other: How to cook, how to shop sensibly, how to stay sober. They helped each other to get jobs, pay the rent, and get to self-help meetings. Although they didn't get along very well in the beginning, they quickly developed a close bond and watched out for one another. Most importantly, they supported each other while going through the frightening and uncertain process of alcohol and drug addiction recovery.

Larry and I were basically "house parents." We drove the women to various group meetings in town. We held house gatherings once a week, and we worked with them to resolve conflicts which arose. It was our privilege to assist wherever we could.

The women were thankful to have Larry as a fatherly male role model in their lives. In turn they helped him to have greater compassion for women and to better understand women's unique issues.

I treasure the memories formed at Triangle House. The first Thanksgiving there, the women all pitched in to prepare dinner and called me for tips on cooking the turkey.

The first Christmas at the house was very special to watch. The "girls" (as I lovingly called them) decorated the tree, baked cookies, and exchanged simple but meaningful gifts. It was heart-warming to see these women whose lives had been ruled by alcohol and drug abuse now behaving like little children thoroughly enjoying themselves on Christmas morning.

Judy helped run the house and always oversaw matters whenever Larry and I left on trips. I want to thank her for everything she did, and I also thank the two ladies who assisted Judy in our absence.

And to the women who courageously faced recovery at Triangle House, thank you! You helped me more than you'll ever know.

Looking back, I realize that Larry and I opened the sober living home during one of the most chaotic times in our lives when Larry was newly sober and I was going through a divorce. I'm sure this was no coincidence. Being immersed in work that benefited others made it much easier to get over our own hurdles.

Today, I am humbled and thankful that Triangle House truly benefited some of these dear women, as told in their own words in the next paragraphs. My wish is that there would be more sober living homes to support people who are struggling to combat alcoholism and drug addiction.

A well-kept, two-story, blue-gray house in a sedate little neighborhood, in the remote small town of Desert Hot Springs, California. There were women of all ages, shapes, sizes, and ethnic backgrounds parading in and out of this house with no seeming rhyme or reason to their routine. This was definitely no ordinary house and these were definitely no ordinary women. This was a sober living home for women new in recovery for drug and alcohol addiction. Women struggling for their lives, their sanity and most of all their sobriety, for without that the rest was hopeless. Struggling to recover that spark of light that they could only dimly remember and prayed was not just a dream from the distant past.

Triangle House was different from treatment centers in that we girls were self-governing. I use the term "girls" because we may have looked like women from the outside but in reality, we were little girls, and scared little girls at that.

We had a set of house rules as guidelines and a house meeting once a week that Judy and Sharon attended to assist us in keeping harmony among ourselves and also to keep us aligned with our primary purpose of staying sober under any and all conditions, and to give us a safe place in which to begin our recovery and gradually adapt back into life. The house rules I can remember were: Of course, no drinking alcohol or using drugs; no stealing; no men in the house after 10:00 PM during the week and 11:00 PM on the weekends; no men in our rooms under any circumstances whatsoever; a set number of self-help meetings to attend each week; and a list of house chores that were rotated weekly. Looking back I can see that these were actually rather loose regulations for such a situation, however I felt very threatened by them when I first moved in. The premise of these regulations was to give us a sense of order and structure in our otherwise chaotic, haphazard existences and also to instill in us some sort of sense of responsibility since most of us had none. Today I am grateful for those regulations, they were exactly what I needed.

So here we were, most of us in our twenties or early thirties, all riddled with fear, anxiety, depression, and a downright knack for creating crisis drama in our lives and those about us, all of this coupled with a very intense need to isolate.

Of course what we all needed most was to receive love and attention and to know that we were not alone and that someone cared about us. As we found acceptance for each other, we began to accept ourselves as alcoholics and bit by bit we set about the road to recovery. It was very important in those early days to be with those who were like myself (alcoholic), to know that I was not alone in this disease and that if these people could stay sober, perhaps I could too. There was hope.

We had our normal household disturbances like: Who ate the last piece of pizza? Who forgot to do the dishes? Who is using my toothpaste? Slowly but surely we learned to communicate without tearing each other apart. Very gradually, as we learned that we were more alike than different, we began to bond with each other and to come out of our shells. We had the garage as the designated smoking area. Many nights one or two of the other girls and I would stay up until the wee hours of the morning smoking and talking and smoking and talking, God only knows about what. Most importantly, we were learning about this new way of life called sobriety. Learning that no matter what ,we just didn't drink or use drugs. Drinking had been our solution to everything in the past, so now we had to stay sober long enough to learn that there really were other solutions.

I had one very good friend there and we even carried on our friendship after we left Triangle House. She is no longer with us in body. She died of liver complications due to her drinking years, but she died sober, married to a man she loved, and pursuing her dream of acting. I consider it an honor to have known her. I find it unlikely that we were placed together by mistake.

I don't know if any of the other women I went through the house with are still sober today. I have been sober almost 6 years today and I am grateful to every one of them for being a part of my experience, for whether or not they know it they served me greatly. I couldn't have stayed sober just for myself, but there is something magical and very powerful about doing it together.

I am also grateful to Larry for his financial backing of Triangle House, and also for taking on the unauthorized role of "house dad." He often accompanied Sharon when she stopped by to check on us. Most of us had little idea what it was like to be in the presence of a healthy male, but Larry set a nurturing and caring example for us.

I can't even begin to stress the importance of women like Judy and Sharon for providing such a place as Triangle House and also for being beacons for us of what a sane and fulfilling life might look like. These were women much further down the road of recovery reaching out a hand to us who were taking our first steps on that journey. They had some idea as to what we would face on that journey, and they took us by the hand and instilled within us the hope that we could make it as well. Patience and tolerance, they must have had a double dose of to be able to deal with women like us. Yet someone had had it for them once upon a time, so they lovingly passed it along to us. These women showed me that being a woman was something that could be done with self-respect, pride and honor for one-self and for others. One of my friend's famous quotes was, "Greta, happiness doesn't just land on you, honey, it comes from right living." I am sure she had no idea how profound that statement was for me. It was pro-found for me then and still is today. I guess truth doesn't change with time.

With this I close. Thank you Sharon and Larry. Thank you Judy. Thank you Triangle House. I couldn't have made it without you.
—Greta

The Triangle House had that feeling of home from the moment I walked through the doors. This was "sober living," a real introduction back into the real world (with support). What I learned in the house will stay with me the rest of my life.

First I found other women who felt as I did. I learned to respect others and to be respected. I learned that no matter what I must be honest with myself and with others or it will kill me. I found that I could trust myself and I was someone: Someone who deserved love and happiness.

—Gae

I was having difficulties in quite a few areas of my life. Financially, mentally, emotionally, and spiritually, I had lost contact with my self-help program and everything I had been taught seemed so far away. I was lost. I made myself go to group meetings and in my own way I was reaching out for help. I knew I had to find a safe place to go.

I continued to attend group meetings and was searching for some kind of answer. To my surprise, I found quite a few women were in the same boat as me with very few resources to turn to. I continued to pray and ask God to please show me the way, no matter what. I believe this was when the change started to happen— now I was praying with no conditions.

Then it happened. Someone gave me the phone number for Triangle House. It was a clean and sober living environment for women. A phone call was all I needed to make.

I can't adequately express in words how the house and women there played a critical part in my recovery. I know in unspoken words from the heart that each of us still carries the love shown to us during that time in us today. I do know for a fact that if Sharon had turned me away I would not be where I am today.

My life has gotten better every day, every month, and every year. The secret: "I have returned to the light." Thank you, Larry, Sharon, all the women at the Triangle House, and most of all God, for giving me another chance at life.

—Toni

Chapter 13

Forgiveness

I thank God that my sons have been able to forgive me for the many ways that I harmed them.

Let go and let God
     Is a motto I saw.
It has taken a long time
     To learn to let go and let God.
I held and held on to my past.
     Today I forgive and learn from my past—
I now live by the motto I saw:
     I let go and let God
And enjoy the freedom I sought.
     —Sharon Cook

Healing can never be complete without forgiveness. I have experienced the truth of Jesus' response to Peter's question in my own life:

> *Then Peter came to Jesus and asked,*
> *"Lord, how many times shall I forgive*
> *my brother when he sins against me?*
> *Up to seven times?"*
> *Jesus answered, "I tell you, not seven*
> *times, but seventy times seven."*
>   —Matthew 18:21-22

I know firsthand that forgiving makes a person healthier physically, mentally, and spiritually. Holding on to anger, hate, resentment, and pride deep inside harmed me, keeping me in darkness. Only when I could truly forgive those who hurt me, and forgive myself for having hurt others, did I finally begin to rediscover the child of light within me.

I have forgiven my mother for living in abuse with my

alcoholic father and stepfather, a pattern which I later followed with the men in my life and with my innocent children. I recognize that Mother loved and nurtured me and took the best care of me she could. I love her and I forgive the choices and mistakes she made which affected me. And I very much hope that she forgives me for the hurt I brought into her life. Mother is a great teacher of mine. I thank her and my maternal grandparents for giving me determination and the desire to search for truth.

I also forgave my biological father. As an adult I possess insight into the fears and insecurities which made him run from the responsibilities of parenthood. I thank him and my paternal grandparents through whom I inherited a love for music and art.

I forgave my stepfather, especially since I came to know personally the pain and confusion he felt as an alcoholic. I recognize that he did love me, and he taught me about work ethics and how to bring creativity into the workplace.

I've taken responsibility for my part in the affairs I had, and I forgive the men who used me in those relationships.

I forgive Allen for his part in the failures of our marriage. He was simply trying to do the right things for me and for our children with the knowledge he had at the time. I hope that he forgives me for all the grief and pain I caused him.

After a long time during which I worked through feelings of rage, I was able to forgive Wayne from my heart. Today I have empathy and understanding for him. Both of us were playing a dangerous game of self-destruction when we were together.

It is my desire that Wayne find it in himself to forgive me for the ugly things I did to him. More importantly, I hope that he too, is finding his way out of darkness and into light.

I thank God that my sons have been able to forgive me for the many ways that I harmed them. I am very proud of David and Bob for taking responsibility for their own actions. Bob has been completely clean of drugs for over six years. David has been in a healthy relationship with a loving, caring woman for the past three and a half years. Both of my children have worked out many issues through counseling and are well on their way to finding the child of light within each of them. What a blessing! I honor them for being conscientious adult men able to take honest looks at their lives.

I want to express my sensitivity to those who have experienced rape, incest, or other terrible violations. For these individuals, it may take a long, long time for a sense of forgiveness to develop. It took me years of working through rage, anger and hate to come to the first stages of forgiveness regarding the molestation that took place when I was five years old.

I recall that when I was forty-eight, I sat next to an elderly man and detected that he smelled just like the man who had molested me over four decades earlier. The scent immediately triggered painful memories and caused me to feel tremendous dislike for this stranger next to me who had not done anything to me. That's how powerfully the crime which occurred so long ago continued to affect my life. I could still experience the feelings of being violated as though the molestation had just taken place.

For most of my life I carried with me shame, guilt, and feelings of unworthiness as a result of one man's selfishness and depravity. I finally came to the understanding that he, not I, created the problems. Still, the molestation became my problem to deal with.

I believe I had to feel rage and anger for a long, long time. But the time came when I needed to forgive and to leave behind feelings of shame and unworthiness. I felt freer when I was finally able to do this.

Of all the people I needed to forgive, it was hardest to forgive myself for the pain I caused in others and in myself. I had to first work through guilt and remorse. When I was able to completely accept that God forgave me, I realized that I didn't need to carry a destructive frame of mind with me any longer. I was free to forgive myself.

At last I knew I was worthy to have a joyful life, for finally I grasped that I truly am a child of the awesome God who loves and protects me.

Today, when I sense someone is cruel, mean, or abusive towards me, I remove myself from the situation. I don't need to be a player in the game of destruction. I simply walk away and whisper a prayer for the person trying to hurt me.

I used to fight and argue, but now I strive for peaceful resolutions. When Larry and I have a disagreement, we talk about it and treat each other with respect. On the occasions when our tempers run short and we say things we regret, we are able to say "I'm sorry" to each other from our hearts. We are able to forgive each other.

More and more, we try to resolve our issues before they get out of hand. Sometimes we fail and feelings are hurt. But most of the time we manage to succeed.

Love and forgiveness are the keys to healing. They enable me to continually strive towards living in the light. And the two are intertwined, because forgiveness to me is the ongoing process of learning to love others and myself.

Chapter 14

Back To Nature

Nature is a wonderful teacher. It beckons one to stop and truly look at God's incredible creation.

My heart is full of love for this forest of trees—
    Spruce, aspen, cottonwood stare straight at me.
Snowflakes seek a place to touch down
    As I look up and see them fall from
    Heaven, abound.
Tiny snowflakes fall on the trees of this
Colorado land,
    Painting a majestic picture as I go forth
To visit nature's wondrous joys.
    Thank you, God, for your beauty
Which you show through the nature
that surrounds me
    In this Colorado forest of trees.
    —Sharon Cook

I was praying during a spiritual seminar in 1992 when the still, small voice inside told me that my next teacher would be nature. My "classroom" was to be a breathtaking location by the Red Rock near the Dolores River (which translates to "the river of sorrow") eight thousand feet high in the San Juan mountains of southwestern Colorado.

Larry was amazingly supportive of my desire to continue my spiritual journey in the forest. He sold his home in the desert and we purchased a house alongside the Dolores, spending the ensuing four years there resting, reflecting, listening, and growing virtually in isolation in the wilderness.

I learned how to be still and process the awesome experiences I had in the previous few years. Poetry started to formulate in my mind and flow freely from my fingers each time I sat down to write. I also began to record my life story, my trials and triumphs, which now appear on the pages of this book.

Larry and I had never before experienced such quietness. It seemed that my life until then had been so overloaded with busy-ness that I was unable to block out all the noises from the city filling my head. As a small child, and even as an adult, I often wondered, "How can people ever hear God?" The answer came to me while living in the mountains, where I learned that I needed practice in clearing my mind of everything external and truly listening.

Walking among towering trees in the forest made me cry with joy. It was a sacred place reminding me of church where the beautiful organ sounds invariably moved me to tears.

Now, the silence of the forest was the music feeding my soul. I came to believe that every church and faith that teaches God's love and light is important. People seem to choose the faith they need for their spiritual growth. I respect every church. God and Christ might have different names in other languages or traditions. But I feel we are all brothers and sisters on this challenging journey called life.

Nature is a wonderful teacher. It beckons one to stop and truly look at God's incredible creation. I watched elk and deer pass through our property. Larry and I sat by the river time and time again, letting its tranquility soothe us in the fall and feeling its raging power in the spring. I experienced the changing seasons: The harshness of winter, the renewal of spring, the vitality of summer, the brilliance of fall. I gazed out of our bedroom window and saw aspen leaves transform mountain tops from lush green to fiery gold. The willows, the spruce, the cottonwoods all filled me with praise for our Creator.

Larry and I became very close in this environment, growing as a couple as well as individually. Having been in forestry years earlier, he taught me how to work with the earth. We planted a new forest together from seedling pine trees. It may sound strange, but I talked to each tree and to rocks, flowers, and the river. Doing so helped me connect with all of creation.

Together, Larry and I grew flowers and vegetables. We cleaned the forest on our land. We painted and remodeled our home. We also spent time alone, apart from each other, pursuing individual interests. Larry learned to create with his hands through carpentry while I meditated, prayed, and wrote poetry daily.

As I reflected on the divine interventions that had taken place in my life, the understanding came to me that I had been living in emotional and spiritual darkness. These phenomenal experiences were necessary to grab my attention and yank me away from the grip of darkness (in which I had been denying—to myself—that I had lived). I also realized that I didn't need these intense experiences any longer because my guidance would come from the quiet voice within, what I call intuition or gut-level listening.

But I still pondered my divine interventions with wonder and awe. I thought about Bill Wilson, one of the co-founders of Alcoholics Anonymous. He, too, had a white light experience. I thought about others who have written about their own encounters with heavenly light. How I longed to talk with these individuals, to hear more about their divine experiences.

In the midst of my yearning, I was comforted by a simple yet crucial realization—we have the chance to experience spiritual awakenings each and every day. Hearing a new-born baby, listening to music and hearing music of the heart, watching a child play, seeing character lines in the elderly, listening to their stories of old, reading a book, making someone dinner, laughing at how human we are, noticing a rose, feeling a rabbit's softness, watching a bird build its nest. We do experience spirituality every day, if we take the time to notice. The earth is a playground God has given to us in love. Respecting and taking care of it is our responsibility.

Today I understand that spirituality is a personal experience for each of us. Feeling from the heart is as much a spiritual awakening as the white light experience I had.

Once, I was baking cookies when I suddenly began to weep. I longed to share this beautiful, sacred place with my sons. At that moment, I wanted them to be little children again and to be able to share with them something as simple yet special as baking cookies in this tranquil, healing setting. I was grieving over their lost childhood. At the same time, I was expanding spiritually and healing.

But I am thankful that Bob and David did encounter the child within each of them as adults in Colorado, just as I did. Both of them visited us at our home in the mountains, each time feeling refreshed and revitalized by the natural surroundings.

My youngest stepson died at age twenty-five while Larry and I lived in the wilderness. I loved him so much. I mourned his premature death and wished that he could have run innocent and carefree through these trees as a little boy. My earlier out-of-body experience gave me comfort, though, in the knowledge that his soul was finally free. I held a private and very personal memorial service for him, walking and crying in the forest as I spoke to his spirit.

I am blessed to have spent four years living in the Rocky Mountains. I experienced so many new things—rafting on the river, holding fresh earth in my hands, planting a new forest, feeling cold, soft snow brushing against my cheeks. I marveled at the power of thunder, the force carried by wind, the gentle strokes of a breeze, experiencing each with a new awareness and appreciation.

Larry and I both got further in touch with our spiritual sides. It was a time of growing, learning, and healing for both of us. Our stay next to the Dolores nourished and strengthened us in preparation for our next adventures.

Chapter 15

Return To The Child Within

Today I am thankful to be alive and full of the light from God!

When I was a child
I loved to sing a song, like so:
*   "This little light of mine,*
I am going to let it shine."
*   As I began to grow into adulthood, with time,*
My light began to grow dimmer and dimmer,
*   Until there was a little shimmer.*
With a force of a strong might,
*   The darkness fell on my childhood light.*
There came one quiet night,
*   In my bedroom, with windows tight,*
A great white light.
*   The light took away the darkness that night,*
And led me back with delight.
*   I stay close to the great white light.*
Today I sing my childhood song, with all my might:
*   **"This little light of mine,***
*   **I am going to let it shine."***
*   God, thank you for bringing me*
Back to the child of light.
                    —Sharon Cook

We are back in the warm, invigorating desert in Southern California, living close to where Larry and I first met. Somewhat reluctantly, we sold our property in Colorado—a stressful, trying task, but one from which we emerged with a faith and purpose stronger than ever.

We are proud to say that both of us remain sober—thirteen years for me, five years for Larry—and that we continue to cleanse ourselves in as many ways as we can. Larry quit smoking and we eat natural foods. He has taken up walking and lovingly coaxes me to join him on daily seven-mile treks. It's important for us to build up strength and energy as we embark on a special mission, that of sharing my life story with others. I hope my story helps inspire and empower people to make positive changes in their lives.

Today I am fifty-five years old. As I review my life, I acknowledge that it's been a wild ride! There have been good times, and bad, and there's been a great deal of pain. At one point my soul was nearly dead. But today I am thankful to be alive and full of the light from God!

I have overcome frightening childhood experiences of abandonment, molestation, and physical abuse. I have overcome my own rage, infidelity, and alcoholism one day at a time. I have taken responsibility for my mistakes. I broke free from the stranglehold of darkness and, with God's help, found within myself the special spiritual child whom He lovingly created.

I've been blessed to have many earthly angels in my life. Teachers who encouraged me. Ministers and counselors who intervened to make me look at myself honestly. Therapists who helped me begin to see truths. People I worked with who gave me parties and made me feel special. People in self-help groups who held my hand while I walked through alcohol recovery. People who helped me with everyday living—plumbers, electricians, motel maids, carpenters, doctors, nurses, garbage collectors, to name a few.

My attorney, who was honest with me and compassionate through the difficult times during my divorce. A special female friend who listened to me day in and day out in my darkest hours. Strangers who acknowledge me through a smile. Little children who bring tears of joy to my eyes as I watch them happy at play. These are but a few of my earthly angels. We are all important to each other.

I am ever thankful to be free at last, free to be the me I was meant to be. Through love, forgiveness, divine guidance, determination, and support, I've come a long way in healing myself, in becoming the spontaneous, curious child that was lost, and in returning to the child of light. But I know that I'm not extraordinary in these accomplishments. I know that *anybody* can turn her or his life around as I did using the God-given power that resides in *each and every one of us.*

I've known many people who have experienced wealth and material gain but still feel empty inside. I've seen some of them eventually begin a journey to find their spiritual paths, and thus start to feed their souls and feel again.

It doesn't matter who you are, it doesn't matter how hopeless your situation may seem, it doesn't matter how far gone you are—*you can change.* I did, and look where I've been in my life.

Whether you are caught in the clutches of alcoholism, drug addiction, eating disorders, sex addiction, gambling addiction, or living with someone who is practicing destructive behavior, *there is hope for a better life.* And there are many ways to attain it. I prayed and meditated. I found people, books, and resources who helped me.

You and I are special children of God's light, just as is everyone on this earth, given free will. I had to learn to use my will wisely and to choose to live in Christ's light.

Recovery of the mind, body, and spirit is a long process, often trying, frustrating, frightening, agonizing. But it's worth the effort. I now possess inner peace, strength to endure life's troubles, the ability to love and forgive myself and others, the desire to live joyfully and abundantly, and an uncompromising faith in light and love. I have rediscovered the important child of light within me. It is my desire that we all find the light within ourselves.

Epilogue

Woman Of Love

I am a woman who has many identities.
  My name is ______________, given to me at birth.
I am many skin colors and express my uniqueness
  In my physical appearance.
I speak different languages.
  The language of feelings I recognize as universal.
I am a daughter, a daughter-in-law, a wife, a lover,
    a partner,
  A mother, a mother-in-law, a sister, and a sister-in-law.
I am a loyal friend, a listener, an advisor,
  A comforter, and a talker.
I am patient and lose my patience.
  I am spontaneous and lovable.
I am caring, generous, and trusting.
  I am honest and perfect.
I am a child of God.
  I am curious, a moon and star gazer, a traveler,
A reader, a student, and a teacher.
  I am interested in nature and people,
    observing how they work.
I love nature and people.
  I am empathetic and physically healthy.
I am Life.
  I am a citizen of the Universe, resident of Mother Earth.
I live in my special country, city, and town.

I am a hard worker, a banker, a homeowner, a landlord,
A diplomat, a cook, a nurse, and a homemaker.
  I am an artist, a dancer, a musician, and a
    drama director.
I am an adventurer in Life.
  I am spiritual, a philosopher, and a psychologist.
I am sensual and have passion for all creations.
  I am a little girl who needs nurturing,
    a woman who nurtures.
I am changing every day, adding to and letting go.
  I am growing, and I am strong.
I am a protector, sensitive, and speak my truth.
  I am realistic, idealistic, and assertive.
I am irrational and rational.
  I am intuitive, private, a daydreamer, and playful.
I am a miracle.
  I am a woman on a spiritual path of life.
I AM LOVE.
		—Sharon Cook

Appendix A

Alcoholism In Society

by Sharon Cook

(Written during Sharon's schooling in drug and alcohol counseling.)

Causes of Alcoholism In Society: Biological—the Family Connection

What causes alcoholism? Researchers today have some pretty good ideas. Studies have shown that alcoholism runs in families. Family histories taken from patients indicate that 95% of the time a close relative also had a drinking problem. Usually, when there is one alcoholic in the family more are found in the background. Heredity studies done worldwide show that genetics are more significant in determining whether or not someone will become an alcoholic than any other single factor examined, and more significant than any combination of social or environmental factors examined. Some people are predisposed to alcoholism because of their heredity, and if they start drinking they run a high risk of developing the disease.

When scientists notice a family predisposition toward a disease, they look for some abnormality in body chemistry. What about the body chemistry of alcoholics? In just these past ten years, it may have been discovered.

In Houston, Texas, a medical scientist named Virginia Davis was doing cancer research on human brains. Many of the brains she analyzed came from homeless alcoholics who had died on the streets.

While discussing some of her findings with other doctors, Ms. Davis commented, "You know, I never realized these people used heroin as well as booze."

The doctors chuckled. They told her that these individuals could not have used heroin—they could barely afford a bottle of cheap muscatel. Puzzled, Ms. Davis went back to her lab. She then realized that she had discovered in the brains of these chronic alcoholics a substance that is closely related to heroin. Long known to scientists, this substance is called tetrahydroisoquinoline, or THIQ. When a person shoots heroin into his body, some of it breaks down and turns into THIQ.

The people in Ms. Davis' study hadn't been using heroin; they were alcoholics but not drug users. How did THIQ get into their brains?

When a normal adult drinker takes in alcohol, it is very rapidly eliminated at the rate of about one drink per hour. The body first converts the alcohol into something called acetaldehyde. This is very toxic, and if it were to build up inside us, we would get violently sick and die. But our bodies help us to get rid of acetaldehyde very quickly, efficiently changing it into acetic acid, (more commonly known as vinegar), and then changing it into carbon dioxide and water which are eliminated through the kidneys and lungs. This is what happens with normal drinkers.

This also happens with alcoholic drinkers, but what Ms. Davis discovered, which has been confirmed since, is that something additional happens in the alcoholic: A very small amount of poisonous acetaldehyde is not eliminated. Instead, it goes to the brain where, through a complicated biochemical process, it winds up as THIQ.

There are three interesting things about THIQ. First, it is manufactured in the brain, and it only occurs in the brain of an alcoholic drinker. It is not produced in the brain of the normal social drinker of alcohol. Second, THIQ has been found to be highly addictive. It was tried experimentally on animals during the second Word War as a pain killer substitute to the highly addictive morphine. THIQ was a good pain killer, but it could not be used on humans as it turned out to be much more addictive than morphine. Scientists then forgot about it for many years.

The third fascinating item about THIQ also concerns addiction. There are certain kinds of rats that cannot be made to drink alcohol. Put them in a cage with a very weak solution of vodka and water, and they will refuse to touch it. They will literally thirst to death before they succumb to drinking alcohol. But if you take the same kind of rat and put a minute quantity of THIQ into the rat's brain with one quick injection, the animal will immediately prefer alcohol over water. It will run across the cage to get to that the alcohol solution. In fact, it will prefer stronger doses of alcohol over solutions heavily diluted with water. So a teetotaling rat is turned into an alcoholic rat with a tiny amount of THIQ.

A biological basis of the disease of alcoholism, then, has been discovered and has been shown to be potentially very important.

Personality

Personality factors have been long thought to play a role in tendencies towards alcoholism, but it has been difficult to pin down just what personality factors are involved. Clinical observations and studies point to many different characteristics.

This has led some investigators to conclude that there must be many personality types susceptible to the disorder, having in common some sort of maladjustment. Others instead believe that there exists an "alcoholic personality." A large number of studies of pre-alcoholics, college problem drinkers, and young heavy drinkers indicate that these individuals are active, aggressive, impulsive, antisocial, thrill-seeking, restless, show marked sexual activity, and show a seeming lack of concern for others combined with an extroverted social nature. There are two competing theories that try to explain these observations.

The dependency theory and the power theory both accept this characterization of the pre-alcoholic, but they differ on its interpretation. The power theory holds that the aggressive and assertive, thrill-seeking and antisocial activities of pre-alcoholics are manifestations of a concern with power. They want power but feel weak and drink to feel powerful. The dependency theory sees the activities and aggression as cover-ups for underlying dependency. They drink in order to satisfy dependency needs. The power theory predominates in many circles.

Sociological Factors

Studies of cultural, ethnic, and religious groups have shown that different groups have markedly different rates of alcoholism, and that these rates do not necessarily correspond to rates of drinking. One approach to isolating the causes of alcoholism has been to compare groups with high and low rates of alcoholism. It turns out that these groups are markedly divergent on their attitudes concerning drinking. Groups which have high rates of heavy drinking and a low rate of alcoholism have several common characteristics, including:
   a. low social pressure to drink,
   b. negative social sanctions against excessive drinking,
   c. accepting attitudes toward moderate, non-disruptive drinking.

Common characteristics of groups with high rates of alcoholism are, for the most part, opposite from those of moderate drinking, low alcoholism groups, and include:
   a. high social pressure to drink,
   b. lack of consistent social sanctions against excessive drinking, and
   c. personal-effects goals in drinking.

It seems that the attitudes and practices found in groups with high and low rates of alcoholism serve to encourage or discourage heavy drinking and alcoholism.

Effects On Society: Economic Cost Of Alcohol Abuse

The economic cost of alcoholism can take the form of a reduction in vital output due to diminished productivity. The total output of goods and services is less than it otherwise would have been because alcohol abuse has had an adverse effect on the productivity of resources.

The economic cost may also be manifested in the need to produce certain goods and services to cope with the consequences of alcohol abuse and alcoholism. This type of loss might include the extra health care that must be produced to treat alcoholism or illnesses brought about by alcohol abuse.

In 1971 the economic cost due to alcohol abuse and associated with alcohol amounted to some $31.4 billion. Alcohol abuse does indeed have a significant economic impact on society.

Health Problems In Industry

In recent years, top management has become more aware that chronic alcoholism is the end product of an illness among employees which inflicts heavy operational costs on employers during its entire progression. The loss, termed "the billion-dollar hangover," has been estimated at over $1 billion annually for U.S. business and industry.

Impact On Family

One of the worst things about alcoholism is that it leaves its imprint on everyone it touches. The immediate victims are the nation's five to six million citizens now suffering from the disease. But many times that number of wives, husbands, children, employers, and friends of the alcoholic are affected. Possible effects of alcohol abuse include a stunted career, breakdown of family and social life, heavy burdens imposed on children of alcoholics, and endanger-ment of family survival.

Social Response to Alcoholism Recovery—Alcoholics Anonymous

Alcoholics Anonymous (AA) leads the way in recovery. In the late 1930's people who were suffering and dying from alcoholism got tired of going to professionals who could not seem to help them—the alcoholics just kept dying or wound up in asylums or jails. So alcoholics banded together and formed a fellowship to help themselves. They discovered a way to stop dying and to make themselves better.

The first thing that society noticed was that AA people were saying that alcoholism is a primary disease. It is its own disease that causes its own symptoms. That is, it is not itself a symptom of another disease, and AA treated it that way. In 1956 the American Medical Association offi-cially recognized alcoholism as a true disease, an entity of

and by itself, that created its own problems, its own symptoms, and had its own treatment. The AMA published this
view in a major paper. This led to legislation that required
hospitals to admit alcoholic patients, whereas before they
had not wanted anything to do with "those drunks."

Treatment and Treatment Centers

Treatments of alcoholism have tended to be based on
one of two common policies. Some treatment centers, like
some private practitioners, specialize in single modality,
conditioned reflex, behavior modification, group therapy,
psychodrama, individual counseling, diet control, or any
other out of dozens of techniques. Recent national surveys
indicate that a community alcoholism rehabilitation program needs to have a variety of methods and resources
available. But effectiveness does not require exposing every
patient to all the possible treatments. Instead, adopting a
social-systems approach, a community-oriented program
should take into account the differences among the
patients, as well as the interactions of the several compo-
nents in the society, and seek to fit the appropriate treatment to each individual.

An essential first level of treatment is detoxification for
the acutely intoxicated person. AA often participates in the
process. After detox, in-patient care and also out-patient
care can be provided. General psychiatric clinics with private practitioners with special interests and skills in treating
alcoholics can be helpful.

Halfway House

This type of facility is for individuals who can maintain employment with proper supervision but who require continuous support except while at work. A facility like this can also be used for the treatment of an alcoholic whose family environment has been one of the contributing factors to his alcoholism. While the patient is at the facility, the family should be educated on alcoholism. Once rehabilitated physically and emotionally, the patient can often return to his home to resume a happy life.

Rehabilitation Center

For the individual in whom alcoholism has advanced to the point where he needs very long periods of intense therapy, a rehabilitation center can be of great help. This center would be for patients with chronic conditions, and should offer complete supervision and medical care. It is essential to return such patients to good physical health, and this often takes a long time.

Summary

The treatment of alcoholics is not an isolated effort left to the alcoholism establishment. It is an effort that requires the coordination and cooperation of caregiving institutions. The institutions must all play a part in the readjustment of alcoholics. It may well be that the treatment of alcoholics is also a part of the government apparatus devoted to giving care to individuals in need and to assist those in need of reintegration into society.

References

Cull, John G. and Hardy, Richard E., <u>Alcohol Abuse and Rehabilitation Approaches</u>, Charles C. Thomas Publisher, Springfield, Illinois, 1974.

Hafen, Brent Q. and Brog, Molly G., <u>Alcohol</u>, West Publishing Company, St. Paul, 1983.

The Christopher D. Smithers Foundation, Inc. ed., <u>Understanding Alcoholism</u>, Charles Scribner's Sons, New York, 1968.

Berry Jr., Ralph E. and Boland, James P., <u>The Economic Cost Of Alcohol Abuse</u>, The Free Press, New York, 1977.

Ohlms, David L., "The Disease Concept Of Alcoholism,"(booklet), Gary Whiteaker Company, Belleville, Illinois, 1983.

Rubington, Earl, <u>Alcohol Problems and Social Control</u>, Charles E. Merrill Publishing Company, Columbus, Ohio, 1973.

Pattison, Mansell E., et. al., <u>Emerging Concepts Of Alcohol Dependence</u>, Springer Publishing Company, New York, 1977.

Block, Marvin A., <u>Alcoholism, Its Facets and Phases</u>, The John Day Company, New York, 1965.

Chafetz, Morris E. and Demone Jr., Harold W., <u>Alcoholism and Society</u>, Oxford University Press, New York, 1962.

Bourne, Peter G. and Fox, Ruth, <u>Alcoholism Progress in Research and Treatment</u>, Academic Press, New York, 1973.

Appendix B

From Generation To Generation

by Graciela Sholander

(First printed in the *Rays of Hope* newsletter)

In the past, I've had a tough time accepting the words of the second commandment in Exodus 20. God says, *"You shall not make for yourself an idol,"* and later, *"You shall not bow down to them or worship them,"* which I understand. But then, Moses tells us that God goes on to say:

"For I, the Lord your God, am a jealous God, punishing the children for the sin of the fathers to the third and fourth generation of those who hate me, but showing love to a thousand generations of those who love me and keep my commandments."

Is this fair? Would God punish somebody for what his father or grandmother or great-grandfather did? This seems to contradict so many other Bible truths.

Psalm 145, verses 17-18, reads, *"The Lord is righteous in all his ways and loving toward all he has made. The Lord is near to all who call on him, to all who call on him in truth."*

This makes more sense to me. After all, each of us is a child of God. He loves every one of us and gives us the freedom to choose to follow Him or to go against Him. We are judged according to what we've done or failed to do, according to our beliefs and thoughts and motives—not what our ancestors did or taught. For instance, God doesn't judge the son of a cocaine dealer any harsher than he judges the son of a hospice worker. If both cry out to God for help, both will be answered by a loving God.

So, what in the world is God saying through His second commandment?

I think that He's pointing out that our thoughts and actions carry a lot of weight. They propagate through distance and time, affecting each person we come into direct contact with as well as unseen future generations.

I do not believe that God purposely sets out to punish the son of a junkie, the daughter of a swindler, the grandchild of a sadist. But they are punished, not through God, but through the legacy that's passed down.

In our society we see families who quarrel over petty matters, full of anger and envy. Racists who pass down hateful beliefs to their offspring. Young mothers with five children from five different men, whose own daughters become pregnant at age twelve. Violent gang bangers who put their tough exteriors aside for a moment to reveal the troubled little children inside suffering from neglect—or worse. Alcoholic and drug addicted parents who abuse their children.

It goes on, and on, and on.

These individuals are showing by their actions that they really don't love God. They "bow down" to idols that take the form of hatred, cynicism, neglect, apathy, violence, self-pity, anger. And, tragically, their offspring suffer, often repeating the negative patterns they've learned from their families.

So I no longer question the second commandment. When we love God and put Him first, our hearts overflow with love that extends to future generations. But when we turn our backs to God and become drug addicts, alcoholics, workaholics, absentee parents, delinquents, and abusers, we hurt not only ourselves but our children, and their children, and their grandchildren. It's that simple.

Notes And Comments

by Sharon Cook

One of the strongest belief systems passed down from generation to generation is the denial of repeating patterns in families. Educating individuals and families is a key to help break the denial system.

A few of the systems which families get trapped in are alcoholism, drug addiction, workaholism, eating disorders, sexual addiction, and gambling, just to name a few. These systems lead to such miseries as anger, hate, greed, lust for power and control, racism, and the blame game.

To be able to step out of the family denial system and take a straight, honest look at the situation is a sign of courage. I appreciate those individuals and families who have taken responsibility for themselves to stop repeating the destructive patterns and have thus come out of darkness and back into light.

Appendix C

Words From My Sons

The Years When Mother Was Married To My Father

Mother was in her early twenties when David and I were born. She was a people-person, always involved in a wide variety of interests. With my father working most of the time, it felt like David, Mother, and I were the "Three Musketeers." From her, we received a great deal of love and we were taught to be caring young men and to not be afraid to show emotion.

Mom made sure to involve David and me in church activities. I received my spiritual base during this period along with my love of family, God, people, and myself.

I don't remember my parents ever arguing in front of my brother and me. Months before my mother asked my father for a divorce, she took David and me out to dinners during which she explained what was going to happen. David and I cried a lot; both of us were scared. We only knew this lifestyle—what was it going to be like after the divorce? Where were we going to live? Most of all, we were scared of losing the family.

The day she told my father she wanted a divorce, David and I were in our bedrooms. We both knew what was happening but we didn't talk about it. My father came and held both of us. It was the first time I saw him cry. I did feel his heart breaking; I knew he loved her very much. Mom knew we loved our father, and she never blamed him for the breakup. She knew he was a good man, but simply her path was—and needed to go— in another direction.

Since my father taught David and me to always treat my mother with respect and as a lady, we were both very protective of her even at the ages of ten and twelve.

Destruction

I feel the only reason we survived the following years is thanks to the spiritual base we received as children.

After the divorce, Mother changed. She always made sure David and I felt secure and were loved, but her personal life changed. She went wild: Late nights, drinking, smoking. I had never seen this side of her before. I began to feel very angry. Mom was dating the man who became her second husband. From the beginning, he and I did not get along. I did not like the change in my mother, and I blamed him for it. He didn't seem to understand that David and I were very close to our mother, and I felt as though he was trying to push us away from her.

Throughout the years after she married my stepfather, Mom's drinking continued to escalate. She and her husband fought all the time, violent fights. One memory I still have not been able to erase from my mind is seeing my mother's blood all over the kitchen floor. I think I went into shock after that night. I never was the same again.

Through my teenage years, the drinking and violence continued. I felt my only relief was to turn to drugs. The drugs masked my feelings and blinded me to what was happening around me.

My mother was no longer the mother I knew. Many times she sat up all night drinking alone. Not only was she losing her physical beauty to alcohol, but her spiritual beauty was fading as well. The only thing I could do at that time was to save myself. My stepfather by this time was starting to hit me, so I left home a few months after turning eighteen.

New Beginnings

I remember Mom asking me if I felt she had a drinking problem. My standard answer was no. I knew the truth but could not bring myself to tell her. It was a great relief for David and me when she finally admitted her problem and went in for treatment. I feel it took several years before I knew she was sincere about her recovery program. Most of my anger was rooted in seeing what she had done to herself. I cried so many times wondering why she did this to herself. It has taken years to erase all of the bad memories.

But Mom did recover her insight and regain her self love. It's been something of a domino effect. After Mom became sober she gave David and me the strength and courage to look at our own lives and to ask for help. She was able to break the chain. Now we are all on the road to recovery.
—Robert

I stayed in my mother's and stepfather's household until I was twenty-three in order to protect her. I finally left home after my stepfather came after me, and I wanted Mom to leave, too. So many times I tried to get her out of the abusive situation she was in. For many years I felt like I had failed because she stayed behind.

Within a month after I left home, she decided to get sober. I was very hurt; why couldn't she have made the decision years earlier, when Robert and I were still with her? For a few years, I didn't trust her. I simply didn't believe that she would stay with the recovery program, based on what I had experienced living with her and her second husband.

But in time, I came to see that she was committed to changing her life and to remaining sober. Today I regret that I did not back her up in her critical early years of sobriety. I guess I was too busy watching out for myself to be there for her.

Mother never gave up on Robert and me. Ultimately

she has inspired us, because she stuck by her words and never went back. And she never stopped talking to us about recovery, never lost hope that we, too, would take the necessary steps to correct our lives. She gave us the strength to take a good look at ourselves and to realize that we needed to get help.

In my own case, I had to lose everything—my first marriage, my job, my home—in order to ultimately win. It was a tough lesson to learn, but I had to hit bottom before I could turn my life around. Mother triggered that turning point; she kept talking and talking to me until it finally clicked that I needed to make drastic changes in my life.

Today, I trust her fully. I think she is an amazing woman, and she is not only my mother but also a best friend, someone with whom I can talk about anything. I know there's nothing Mom wouldn't do for Robert or me.

I feel like everything has been going my way these past three years. It's amazing how God opens doors when someone is really trying to improve. I am with a woman that I love very much, and I feel richer in every way than I've ever felt before. I am thankful for the numerous wonderful things in my life, and for my renewed closeness with Mom and my reinforced faith in God.

Belief and trust in God, more than anything else, is what helped me endure and overcome my past.
—David

Appendix D

Poems From The Heart

"The Lady Who Stole My Dad" was written on May 22, 1987, by Anna Raye Skaggs, one of Sharon Cook's cousins. It demonstrates how alcoholism often prevails within a particular family, in this case plaguing Sharon and, indirectly, her cousin Anna, among others.

The remaining poems in this section were written by Sharon Cook.

The Lady Who Stole My Dad

She started her flirting
at a very young age.
Her life story
could fill more than a page.

She kept my dad
away from home,
leaving us
to cry alone.

The disappointments
and sorrows she cast
left their mark
which will forever last.

She changed our family
and tore us apart.
Her intoxicated spell
made him feel so smart.

Yet the queen called alcohol
left a memory so sad.
That's why I call her
"The Lady Who Stole My Dad."

God's Love

God's love is everywhere,
Look, look, see—is it over there?
God's love is inside.
Open up your heart and abide.
He is there at the very start.
Christ said, "Knock at your door of hearts."
Christ's Light is brighter than the stars,
The Light has been there from the very start.
Open up your door of hearts.

My Mother

Her name is Pearl.
Her skin is white like the glistening snow.
She is a woman with a little girl inside.
When she talks of her past her eyes dance like
sparkles in snow.
My mother has stood tall like spruce trees throughout
*   her life.*
Her life has moved like clouds in the sky,
Through winter, summer, spring, and fall.
She has moved quick like the birds and squirrels
gathering food for her brood.
God has provided her with warmth
as the sun gives out its warmth to all.
She has given sunshine out to all, even in the fall.
Yes, my mother is like nature.
She is all seasons, winter, summer, spring, and fall.
She is a beautiful Child of God who stands tall.

Magical Works Of Light

The Colorado forest inspires me.
  The snow glistening like a magical star.
A breeze, blowing, sparkles of snow light.
  I feel nature and see the snow and forest afar—
This world, too, is inside of me.
  A breeze in me touches my spiritual light,
I know it is God's might.
  A bird comes forth to offer his sight.
He, too, knows of God's Great Might.
  Thank you, God, for allowing me to peer
Into your magical works of light.

Icicles

I remember as a little girl
  Putting icicles on a Christmas tree,
    My mother told me to put them on straight.

She said, "My child, not like a curl."
  Now as a woman learning from nature
    I see the icicles hang from the tall spruce trees.

Watching them form, from the touch of their clarity,
  Forming beautiful and dancing gracefully,
    They are surrounded by nature's simplicity.

Where have the icicles gone from the tree?
  Back to water and to nurture me.

Larry

Life may seem difficult, but we have each other tonight.
What a gift to have someone
to comfort with each night.
As we give thanks we realize not everyone
is as fortunate as us.
We are special. I love you with all my might.

To The Degree Of Truth

I can be of service to God, myself, and others
To the degree that I practice the truth.
As I learn more truths it is my responsibility
To live those truths and practice them.
It is my responsibility to learn God's
truth and to practice it
So that I may serve God, myself, and society.
Therefore it is I who changes to accept more
truths of the universe,
God's Laws. Then to be able to practice to
degrees of truth will be
Returning to where I am God's partner
in the Universe and Love.
What an adventure—what more to have in life?

My Sons

Robert and David are joys to me
They touch my heart with their special laughter
Watching them grow has been joyful, painful,
and sad,
Their lives have followed part of my path.
They now take responsibility for the past.
I thank God for these special sons.
They are my children, friends, and we have fun
Learning to love each other, as mother and sons—
A gift from God, who is the all-powerful One.
Their lives are on the right path toward
light and love
I thank God for answering from above
For David and Robert are surround by Christ's
Light and Love,
Thank you my sons, for straightening your paths.
For Light is at the end of our struggling paths.

My Great Creator

My Great Creator, how beautiful thou art!
*   You are everywhere I look today,*
*   High and low, from breath to breadth.*
The love you give to us is all there is.

It has taken many years to discover your love
*   Which the Master taught centuries ago.*
*   Thank you, my beloved Father, King.*
May I cherish the love you have given me
*   and express it to all living creations.*

Thank you for my gift of life.
*   I truly adore thee, my Creator and King.*
*   I love you at last!*
My heart sings forth a joyful noise unto my Lord.

God's Natural Christmas Tree

I am today a beautiful Christmas tree,
 natural and alive.
I have gifts under my tree;
The gifts are for those who have supported
 and loved me.
My top has an angel on it which is Christ.
There are ornaments which sparkle with excitement
As they dance around on my branches.
Some are old, some are new; they represent
my personality.
I have discarded ones that were not of any use,
That weighed my branches down.
There are candy canes on my branches
 waiting for children
To pick off and enjoy my gift of love.
My lights shine for all those who want to see.
The nativity scene is underneath me,
God's gift to all sending life, love, hope,
And throughout my tree and on to other trees.
I am not ashamed of how I look.
I don't have to hide in the forest anymore.
God wanted this tree to be taken from the forest.
God planted a seed.
He chose certain people to water and nourish it.
God took me home and decorated me.
I am at last God's Natural Christmas Tree.

> *But for the Grace of God*
> *Thank you God for those who have*
> *Nurtured me and help me to heal.*

Appendix E

Self-Help and Anonymous Groups

National Council on Alcoholism & Drug Dependence
(800) 622-2255
(800) NAC-CALL

National Domestic Violence
(800) 799-7233
(800) 799-SAFE
TDD: (800) 787-3224

National Mental Health Consumer Self-Help Clearinghouse
(800) 553-4539
Hearing Impaired: TTY1-215-751-9655

National Youth Crisis Hotline
(800) 448-4663

National AIDS Hotline
English: (800) 342-2437
Spanish: (800) 344-7432
TDD: (800) 243-7889

**Childhelp/IOF Foresters
National Child Abuse Hotline**
(800) 422-4453
(800) 4-A-Child

Look in your phone book for these and other "anonymous" groups:

> Alcoholics Anonymous (AA)
> Al-Anon
> Adult Children of Alcoholics
> Narcotics Anonymous (NA)
> Overeaters Anonymous
> Eating Disorders Anonymous
> Cocaine Anonymous
> Sex Anonymous (SA)
> Gamblers Anonymous
> Debtors Anonymous
> Nicotine Anonymous

Your local phone book may also list treatment centers, counseling centers, and mental health associations in your area.

About the Authors

Sharon L. Cook is a motivational speaker, author, and poet. She is frequently a guest speaker on radio shows and at various organizations. Her past experience includes working in real estate, counseling in substance abuse, and achieving her goal of opening a sober living home.

Together with Larry, who provides moral support and manages the business side, she is traveling across the country to speak about her life story in many communities. It is Sharon's desire to share her experiences, strength, and hope with others.

Graciela B. Sholander is a freelance writer published in several magazines, including Women's Circle, Family Magazine, and many regional parenting, travel, inspirational, and women's publications. Before becoming a writer and an at-home parent, she worked as an electrical engineer.

With loving support from her husband, Kevin, a computer engineer who reviews her manuscripts and creates accompanying computerized art, she is working on other books and articles. She shares her views in an upcoming book, *Together We Are*.

To reach any of the contributors to this book, write to:

> Triangle Publishing House
> PO Box 272654
> Fort Collins, CO 80527-2654

If you enjoyed this book, please share it with a friend.

Ordering Information

To order a copy of *Return to the Child of Light*, by Sharon L. Cook, send $14.95, plus $3.00 postage and handling, along with your name and address to:

> Triangle Publishing House
> PO Box 272654
> Fort Collins, CO 80527-2654

(Colorado residents please add 6.25% sales tax.)